IN
THE
RING
OF
FIRE

Other Works by James D. Houston

FICTION
Between Battles
Gig
A Native Son of the Golden West
Continental Drift
Gasoline
Love Life
The Last Paradise

NONFICTION
Farewell to Manzanar
(with Jeanne Wakatsuki Houston)
Open Field (with John R. Brodie)
Three Songs for My Father
Californians: Searching for the Golden State
One Can Think About Life after the Fish Is in the Canoe
The Men in My Life

EDITOR
Writing from the Inside
California Heartland: Writing from the Great Central Valley
(with Gerald Haslam)
West Coast Fiction

IN THE
RING OF FIRE

A PACIFIC
BASIN JOURNEY

BY JAMES D.
HOUSTON

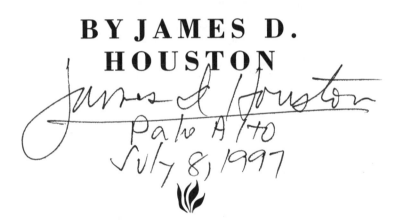

James D. Houston
Palo Alto
July 8, 1997

MERCURY HOUSE · SAN FRANCISCO

Published in the United States of America by Mercury House,
San Francisco, California, a nonprofit publishing company devoted to the free exchange of ideas and guided by a dedication
to literary values.

United States Constitution, First Amendment: Congress shall
make no law respecting an establishment of religion, or prohibit-
ing the free exercise thereof; or abridging the freedom of speech,
or of the press; or the right of the people peaceably to assemble,
and to petition the Government for a redress of grievances.

Mercury House and colophon are registered trademarks of
Mercury House, Incorporated.

Printed on recycled, acid-free paper and manufactured in the
United States of America.

Maps, design in Adobe Bulmer, and typesetting
by Thomas Christensen.

Portions of this material have appeared previously in such pub-
lications as the *New York Times,* the *Los Angeles Times Sunday
Magazine, Image: The Magazine of the San Francisco Examiner,
San Francisco Focus, Faultline, Common Boundary, Wild Duck
Review, Honolulu Magazine,* and *Manoa: A Pacific Journal of
International Writing.*

Library of Congress Cataloguing-in-Publication Data:
Houston, James D.
In the ring of fire : a Pacific Basin journey / by James D. Houston
p.   cm.
ISBN 1-56279-100-1 (alk. paper)
1. Pacific Area—Description and travel. 2. Houston, James D.—
Journeys—Pacific Area. 3. Pacific Area—Civilization. I. Title.
DU23.5.H68   1997
909'.09823—DC21   97-2172
                                        CIP

9 8 7 6 5 4 3 2 1
FIRST EDITION

Facing west from California's shores,
Inquiring, tireless, seeking what is yet unfound,
I, a child, very old, over waves, toward the house of maternity, the land
of migrations, look afar,
Look off the shores of my Western sea, the circle almost circled . . .

— Walt Whitman, from *Leaves of Grass* (1860)

CONTENTS

IN
THE
RING
OF
FIRE

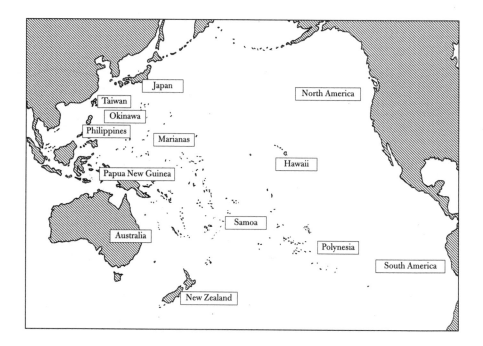

The Pacific Region.

AIRLINES
AND
BLOOD LINES

Outside my attic window I can see it, gray and glassy under a high-hanging fog. By noon the fog will lift, the offshore wind will rise, the surface will turn from slick gray to wrinkled bluish green, then cobalt to the horizon, stretching west. Day after day it stretches, close enough to hear and touch and taste, yet far too vast to know. It glitters and it rumbles and it works on you. It hums, it beckons, inviting, ominous, promising things, always promising.

Ferdinand Magellan named it the Pacific back in 1521. For four-and-a-half centuries or so that's what it was called, the name invoking a realm that included not only the globe's largest body of water, but all the islands the water surrounds and all the places you can reach by sailing or flying across the water. As a zone of exploration, the Pacific still resonates with legendary trips and voyagers—Sir Francis Drake, Captain Cook, Captain Bligh, and Fletcher Christian and Herman Melville and Amelia Earhart.

I'm not certain when the word Rim was added. Sometime in the early 1980s I began to hear it frequently. Adding that word has revealed something about how we see this part of the world, as well as the world in general now. It conjures up another kind of picture, suggesting that the farther side has long ago been reached and charted and that exploration, at least in the earlier sense, has more than been taken care of. Pacific Rim turns our seemingly boundless ocean into an enormous wheel, a mandala of interconnected places.

I have spent most of my life within walking distance of the water, here along the coastal region of California, which is one small segment of the Rim. It has become a kind of borderland, where more and more histories meet, overlap, converge, collide. You feel it in a thousand ways—in the markets, in the restaurants, on the roads, in the martial arts academies, on the all-Asian TV channels where newscasters speak in Mandarin, on the all-Hawaiian music show via FM radio out of Salinas every Sunday afternoon. There is a Samoan center playing for the San Francisco 49ers, and in a town in Los Angeles County there is a Korean-born mayor, and down in the deepest canyon of the Santa Lucia range, in the wilderness behind Big Sur, where wild boar is hunted and lions still roam, there is a zendo, a meditation hall, and a wooden gong hanging from a rope. When you hear the mallet ringing wood on wood in the predawn air, you could swear you're somewhere in the mountains of Japan.

Rise from your cabin bed, for an early stroll, and inside the zendo you hear chanting in Japanese, as novices repeat the sutras that get them centered for the day, for the chores that are two things at once: necessary work, and forms of daily discipline, forms of practice. Listen to the sutras. Listen to the scrape of slippers on the swept path. Listen to the mallet chime that marks the progress of the day, and look at the round eyes of the novices. Not an Asian face among them. There are more Zen practitioners in the US now, I've heard it said, than you will find in Japan. At the mountain Zen center, down at the bottom of a fourteen-mile logging road, the abbot in residence is American too, a woman who looks to be in her sixties, with her hair cropped close and her black robes rustling like leaves.

The zendo was recently rebuilt. The cabin you rent, when they open the center for summertime visits, is made of elderly planking that harks back to the days before World War II when the cluster of buildings in this remote and heavily wooded canyon was a hunting and fishing lodge. Before that it was a rustic, backcountry resort. And before that it was a retreat much revered by local tribes who found nourishment and renewal in the natural hot springs. Spanish explorers named the place Tassajara. Springs percolate from underground and flow through tubs now, and into the gushing tumble of the creek, to send up curls of steam where hot meets cold and leave a mineral residue on creek-rolled stones.

Once or twice a year we go down there, my wife and I. For each of us the trip into the Los Padres wilderness is a little pilgrimage to a serene and protected place that is also an emblematic place.

Her background happens to be Japanese. Tubs of hot water always revive connections to her early years growing up near Inglewood, where her father farmed row crops on land now covered by the runways of L.A. International Airport. They had an outdoor tub, a furo, heated from below by a wood-fueled fire. She was the youngest of ten. At the end of the day her family would come in off the fields and gather there to sit and sweat and talk and soak away the aches and pains.

For me, these are trips into the kind of terrain my father and I used to hike through together. He was a man from east Texas who kept rifles and loved to hunt, though I later realized that the chance to get out of San Francisco and wander a while in open country was at least as important for him as bringing down a deer to carry home. I never took to the killing. I'm not sure why. Maybe it was growing up a city kid. Maybe if we had truly needed the meat it would have been a different story. But thanks to him I discovered the many pleasures of the long Coast Range, the boot crunch of soil under still madrones, the curl of rusty bark under arid, pale blue sky.

Somehow all of these things inhabit the atmosphere of Tassajara canyon, where the final edge of America's wilderness meets Asia. Wild boar. Mountain lion. Temple gong. Jay squawk. Creek tumble. Black robe. Morning sutra. Steam curl in morning fog. Madrone and oak and manzanita. Sitting buddha. Logging road.

From canyon to ocean is only ten miles, as the crow flies. I think of it as a Pacific place, one of a number I've had the chance to visit recently and have tried to write about. Some are on this side of the ocean, some are on the other side, some are right out in the middle. I think of this as a book of journeys by a *traveler from the West Coast who has been drawn farther west, looking around, looking for guidance in a vast and various region of the world I feel more and more connected to, looking for ways to see my family and homeland with clearer eyes.*

The idea occurred to me a couple of years ago on a Japanese train. We were moving along the coast of Kyushu, the southernmost island. Blue water surged against black chunks of lava shoreline. We passed the smoking cone of Sakurajima, which had recently spewed a light layer of ash upon the rooftops of the nearest town. I started thinking about the Ring of Fire, as I often do, the great ring of tectonic borderlands, and how the cones and craters and bubbling subterranean waters of Kyushu resemble those along the farther shore—that is to say, this *shore—the one we'd come from and would return to, with its own scheme of fracture lines and hot springs and old cones and dormant craters. I saw that the record I had begun to keep would not only be about Japan. It would roam around the broad basin made of shores and islands, and follow some of the lines that stretch across the water.*

What kinds of lines did I have in mind?

I thought of seismic lines.

I thought of melody lines that fly like birds from shore to shore, the Muzak notes drifting down from the overhead speakers inside the train. "Where or When." "Over the Rainbow." "Do Nothing 'Til You Hear from Me."

I thought of family lines too, and the ways certain people have moved around this ocean.

I thought of Salevaa Atisanoe, who had been on TV again, the wrestler they call Konishiki, center stage in a celebrity fundraiser. They are the quarterbacks, these sumo champs, the Japanese demigods of sport. And Konishiki—while we were living there—was right up on top of the heap, a culture hero, a favored talk-show guest, in his jumbo yukata, his sash, his black hair knotted. That week he happened to be in Tokyo, which is one of three touchpoints that connect the lines of the world he inhabits, his own Pacific triangle.

Konishiki came of age in Honolulu, went to high school there, played football at about half the five-hundred-and-fifty pounds he carries now. His family comes from American Samoa.

I thought of Samoa, a thousand miles below the equator, and then thought of other islands.

Bali.

Java.

Guam.

Saipan, where old battle lines were drawn.

Tinian, where the first atomic bombs were stored.

Okinawa.

Ie-jima.

Pearl Harbor.

I thought of Hawai'i, where all lines seem to intersect. Pacific crossroads. Geological hub. America meets Polynesia there, and Visa cards collide with naming chants.

I thought of my wife's father, Ko Wakatsuki, the man who built an outdoor bathing tub where transoceanic jets now touch down. He stopped in Hawai'i back in 1904. Born on the island of Honshu, eldest son in a samurai family that had fallen on hard times, he took a steamship east from Yokohama at the age of seventeen. He had been to military school and might have become an officer, but he didn't like the marching. He preferred to take his chances in this new land across the Pacific. In Honolulu he got off the ship and lingered a while, looked for work. Young and eager, he picked up a little traveling money and climbed aboard another ship bound for the coast of North America.

And I thought of the day, some fifty years later, when he and I met, for the first and only time.

We were never formally introduced. Jeanne was afraid for me to meet him, knowing how deeply her father would disapprove. By that time both our families had arrived, from their opposite directions, in Santa Clara Valley, and Jeanne and I were enrolled at San Jose State. She had nine brothers and sisters. She was the youngest, and she was the renegade, the first to go to college, the first to date outside the race.

We'd been going together for about a year when I decided, one Saturday afternoon, to drive out to her family's house. She had said she'd meet me in San Jose. For some reason I insisted on picking her up. Maybe I saw this as the chivalrous thing to do. Maybe I knew this was the only way I'd ever have a chance to look him in the eye.

He was working strawberries then. The house was off to the side of his field, among some outbuildings. As I pulled into the yard, he appeared on the porch, in jeans, an old felt hat. I was driving a 1938 Chevy sedan. He looked first at the car, with grave doubt, then at me. He had a thin black mustache, and a weathered, aristocratic face. When I told him why I was there he shook his head and seemed to cough. He stepped down off the porch, stood with his feet planted and his hands on his hips, holding me with his gaze in a way that forced me to look at him.

In that brief exchange, at the edge of his field of immaculately tended berry furrows, I saw a man, or felt the spirit of a kind of man previously unknown to me, a man from Asia. I would later learn that he had lost most of his relatives in the bombing of Hiroshima. Thirty years before I was born he had immigrated to the West Coast, to work, to live, to make a fresh start. He and my father had at least that much in common. His home region was in a deep depression when he left Japan bound for the Land of Promise.

He had worked as a lumberjack, a cook, a farmer, and eventually as a fisherman based at San Pedro. After the attack on Pearl Harbor, in December 1941, he was arrested by the FBI, falsely charged with delivering fuel to enemy submarines off the coast of California. He lost his boat and he lost a career sitting out the Second World War in an internment camp called Manzanar, in the high desert east of the Sierra Nevada range, not far from Death Valley. He had been so scarred by these experiences, he had stopped speaking to Caucasians. It was a point of honor. Now into his yard had come a sun-tanned Anglo fledgling with scales on his eyes and lust in his heart, driving a neglected '38 Chevy and looking for his youngest daughter.

All this was in his face. Though I could not have known it, I must have felt it. I felt something coming from him, and it was not hatred or bitterness. What he projected was the hard-won toughness of a man who had survived everything America and Japan had thrown at him, who had preserved his dignity and found a way to continue.

I never saw him again. The year before we were married he passed away.

But as I came to know the clan he'd left behind, Jeanne's brothers and sisters and their families, and as I learned to be the new uncle to thirty-six nieces and nephews, and heard the many family stories, I often thought about that afternoon, about meeting the man who is the grandfather of our three children. It was a moment of awakening, the beginning of an education that continues to this day. A window had been opened, for the first small glimpse of another place, another way of being in America, and my first glimpse of a life, a history that reached both ways across the water.

❦

Melody lines. Memory lines. Dream lines. Fracture lines. Battle lines and airlines and blood lines. I have tried to follow a few of them here, journeys both outward and inward, forward and backward, always returning home again, as most journeys do. It was the poet T. S. Eliot who said,

> *We shall not cease from our exploration*
> *And the end of our exploring*
> *Will be to arrive where we started*
> *And know the place for the first time.*[1]

FULL-LENGTH MIRROR

I

FUKUOKA, KAGOSHIMA, IBUSUKI, YUFUIN

The same waves wash the moles of the new-built California towns, but yesterday planted by the recentest race of men and lave the faded but still gorgeous skirts of Asiatic lands, older than Abraham; while all between float milky-ways of coral isles, and low-lying, endless, unknown archipelagoes, and impenetrable Japans.

— Herman Melville, *Moby Dick* (1851)

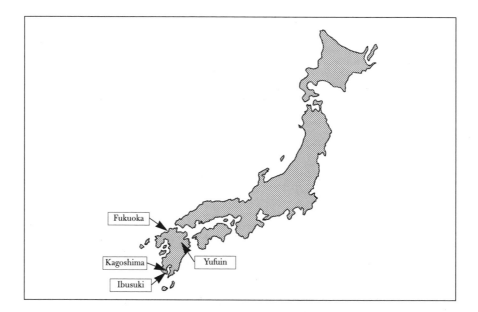

*Japan. Korea is to the west, Russia to the north, the Pacific Ocean
to the east, the Philippine Sea to the south.*

TRAVELING
MUSIC

December 1991. When the traffic light changes, the go sign shows a human figure silhouetted against the green, a white cutout. Three dozen pairs of feet start walking while computerized chimes play the street-crossing tune:

> If a body meet a body,
> Coming through the Rye,
> If a body kiss a body,
> Need a body cry?

You don't hear the words. You only hear the tune that has somehow made its way from the Scots Highlands to a speaker box behind the green light, above this crosswalk in midtown Fukuoka.

"Coming through the Rye" plays on street corners, all through the day and night, traveling music for the multitudes who cross and recross the intersections of this very busy and very international city of a million people, old port city facing north and west toward the tip of Korea. Does anyone recognize the tune? Or know the lyrics? Or care one way or another? Probably not. It is just in the air, first byte from the Global Soundtrack of western favorites that fills the atmosphere.

On the phone to the bilingual travel agent booking my Japan Air flight, if he has to put me on hold, the same chimes fill the waiting time with "Greensleeves," old Elizabethan heartsong:

Alas, my love, you do me wrong
To cast me off so discourteously,
For I have loved you oh so long,
Delighting in your company.

I am only cast off for a few moments. And back he comes, *"Moshi, moshi?"*

DAYS AND NIGHTS
IN FUKUOKA

Fukuoka. City of contrasts. City with a split personality. Or a multiple personality. Like Japan. Like America. Like everywhere you go these days. Is everything dividing against itself? Or dividing in order to recombine? The Japanese are not as Japanese as they used to be. Americans are not as American. Some people say this is what's driving us crazy. They say it's time to let go of some of those precious boundaries we have been clinging to for so long.

Which boundaries? What do I mean by this? It's too soon to say for sure. I am just sitting here in Fukuoka, seven thousand miles from the place I call home. It is fifty years after the bombing of Pearl Harbor, and I am thinking out loud, thinking about Japan and America and the Pacific Rim and the cars we drive and the songs we listen to, and the river that divides this two-hearted city down the middle.

In the old days there were two towns here—to the west of the river, Hakata, a market town; to the east, Fukuoka, the old castle town, where remnants of the castle still stand. As the towns grew, they merged. A name had to be chosen for the new and larger community. Fukuoka won out. But Hakata refused to disappear. A hundred years later this is still the name of the train station. When you travel from Tokyo, five hours south by bullet train, your destination is Fukuoka. Your ticket says Hakata.

At night, down by the river, in the Nakasu district, neon lights glare from the sidewalks to the tops of the many-storied buildings, columns of light, towers and spirals, flashing and pulsing. It is billed as "the largest entertainment quarter in western Japan." Half the street noise comes from *pachinko* parlors crowded with rows of machines that sound like forty cathedral organs gone haywire. The game is a vertical version of pinball, with the balls propelled upward. While lights flicker, you watch the balls drop through a pattern of obstacles, racking up points as they fall. The machines are lined up by the hundreds, like the slots in Las Vegas, with that kind of brilliant, all-night, all-day lighting.

There are also amusement parlors with rifle shoots, video games, the arm-wrestle machine, the claw machine for lifting little furry creatures to the exit chute. Outside, clusters of young men in business suits lunge along in twos and threes, arms around shoulders, laughing in and out of the bars. In the phone booths young women have left photographs taped next to the coin box. They come in multiple copies, with numbers attached. Some are simply faces with inviting smiles, Japanese, Filipina. Some pose in low-cut blouses and miniskirts. Some are nude.

During the day the crowds are found on the other side of the river, in the city's center, called Tenjin, where the big department stores start underground, linked by a network of tunnels and malls that make a city-under-the-city—restaurants, coffee shops, newsstands, boutiques, clothing stores, markets heaped with tangerines and cucumbers, box lunches, chicken teriyaki to go, kimchee, German sausage, sourdough baguettes—all below sidewalk level and tied to the subway system. You can buy French suits, Chinese brocade, Italian pasta, California wine. You can spend the day under there, follow corridors from one tall store to another, take the elevator to the top, then descend again and drop down the long steep escalator to a subway platform that is always clean. No cigarette butts down there, in this country where they go through 322 billion cigarettes a year. No trash on the platform, no graffiti on the walls. And no street crime to speak of. Not here in Fukuoka, at any rate. You can roam around downtown all afternoon, go out for dinner, take the subway home at 11 PM or midnight and walk half a mile across the park, and not give it a second thought.

The Tenjin district takes its name from a small Shinto shrine set back from the city's busiest boulevard. The shrine honors Sugawara Michizane, a famous ruler of the ninth century, later deified and now numbered among the saints. According to the legend, he was on his way to Dazaifu when he saw his reflection in the Shiju River. Later a shrine was erected at the spot and given the name *Suikyo Tenjin,* or "Full-Length Mirror." In 1612 it was moved to the present site. It's small, one story, with a steeply sloping pagoda roof. The narrow courtyard is guarded by lion-dogs and surrounded by red-orange fencing. Three hundred and seventy-five years ago it probably stood out there by itself, with a view of the river. Now it's hard to see. On either side, high-rises have been built right up next to the fencing. They make a classic urban canyon, with shaded walls looming above a torii gate and the thousand-year-old shrine which now looks out across the sidewalk into lanes of endless traffic. At first glance it seems buried, in perpetual shadow, and its name is almost too tempting to leave alone. Isn't this one of those full-length mirrors in which we can see what Japan has been doing to itself? Isn't this a perfect example of the new overwhelming the old? The runaway materialism of the present overwhelming spirituality and the graceful lines of tradition?

Well, yes, it's true. The Tenjin shrine is a mirror for Japan, while the transformation of Japan is itself a reflection, another version of what is going on all around the globe. And yet, in the style and age of these elderly shrines, something else is going on. They are the venerable and bearded elders who bear witness to the midday sounds and swirling sights. Though they appear to be overwhelmed, they have not been neglected. Step past the torii gate, past the fencing and the guardian deities, and you come upon a small and leafless tree that perhaps never sees the sun. Its wintry branches are filled with other leaves. Small strips of white paper have been tied to the twigs and branches, hundreds of prayers and pleas for good luck, good life, good outcome. You see these outside every shrine, large and small. You see them by the thousands, everywhere you go, trees blossoming with white strips tied to the branches.

Outside the shrines there are also public wish boards, prayer boards. For 200 yen you can buy a wooden tablet about the size of a small shirt pocket, with a blessing on one side and with space on the flip side to write out your wish before you hang it on the board—pleas for prosperity, for more money, for better grades in school, for harmony in the family, for safe travel. In our neighborhood everyone is in on this, men and women, young and old. Outside the local shrine, the prayer board is filled with tablets, hundreds of them hanging from little hooks, layer upon layer. This does not mean that all these wish makers are going to church services on a regular basis. But they go *to* the church, the shrine, the altar, giving voice to the heart's desire. Call it faith. Call it ancestry. Call it superstition. The Japanese are very superstitious, and they don't try to conceal it. When the big downtown retailers want to bring in business, it's not enough to drop the prices and announce a sale. You also announce that a fortune-teller is on standby. One department store in Tokyo has been advertising four fortune-tellers at a time. The retailer pays each one forty thousand yen per day, which is about three hundred dollars, and you can't get into the store for the lines of shoppers backed up and waiting for some free advice.

Out here where we are living, in the district called Ropponmatsu, the local shrine is less surrounded, more serene, a little oasis in the midst of a crowded residential neighborhood. High trees make a park that you enter through the timbered frame of an arching torii gate. It's called Gokoku Jinja, a simple building, low and elegant, fronted by a courtyard the size of a soccer field. Between two long and close-cropped lawns, a broad promenade of gravel is raked each day, so that you always see straight tine-marks running the length of the walkway. Some days you will see tire marks cutting through the rake lines. At the end of the tire tracks you are liable to find a car parked right in front of the steps leading to the portico.

I was passing through there yesterday, on my way to the subway station, and came upon a fellow in slacks and windbreaker and running shoes, opening the trunk of a new gray Toyota. His young wife stood nearby, watching. When he had opened the hood and all four doors, a priest came out from under the sloping roof in his white robes and pointed black hat, carrying a scepter with white puffs attached. It looked like a white pompom, which he waved as he slowly walked around the car, chanting softly. He waved it back and forth above the four cylinders of the engine, back and forth in front of each open door, inside the yawning trunk where the spare and the jack are housed. Then he bowed deeply. The owner and the owner's wife bowed. The priest went back inside. I watched the owner close the trunk, drop the hood, close all the doors, climb into his now-secure and well-blessed car, turn it around, and cruise across the long, empty courtyard, out into the Sunday traffic along Kokutai-Doro Road, where he would soon be stopped at an intersection while pedestrians crossed in front of him to the tune of "Coming through the Rye."

The main entrance to these grounds is framed by two single logs maybe five feet thick, set well apart, and soaring to the high carved crosspiece. The logs are old and straight and comforting in the middle of a district where most of the buildings have gone up in the last thirty years or so, concrete buildings filled with small apartments. The logs are smooth and thick and elemental, surviving from some earlier time. They rise above a boulevard rumbling with traffic and seem to point the way toward an adjoining park, much larger, mostly open space, more water than grass, a midcity lake bordered with willows and azaleas and jogging trails. Called *Ohori*, it's modeled after a famous park in China. It's another oasis, with the water at least half a mile across.

In the middle of the lake, three small islands are connected by narrow bridges. The perimeter road makes an oval, wide and flat, where joggers jog from dawn till dark. The women jog alone, or in pairs. The young men sometimes jog in teams of ten or twenty, with a leader calling signals. They jog in the heat, and in the rain, and on days when it's cold enough to snow. On this day in mid-December the air is filled with a yellow light that gives a soft edge to the mountains behind the city. In late afternoon the lake is a window of yellow silver. An old man is walking his dog. Girls are walking home from school in their matching navy blue dresses with white-bordered navy-style collars. From a hundred yards away I hear a tenor saxophone I've heard a couple of times before. Somebody comes out here late in the day to sit alone by the lakeshore and work on a blues riff a little beyond his reach, the high notes squeaking, the lower notes round and full, the same four bars over and over and over, floating above the water.

On one side of this park stand the ruins of Fukuoka Castle. Its foundations cover a high promontory. Like massive stairs they climb the slope. The old retaining walls of fitted stone slant inward. Above the trees behind me, like a glimpse from a samurai film, one square tower still shows, built in 1601 when the legendary Kuroda clan controlled the region.

On the other side of the park, near the subway station, there is a Mister Donut, where you can get a pretty good cup of coffee for under two dollars. It's the best price in town, and that is one reason the place is usually packed, though not the main reason. Mister Donut is the centerpiece of a little cluster of shops called the American Carousel Plaza. Inside, surrounded by booths and tables there is a mini-carousel, four silver poles with two merry-go-round horses on each pole, moving up and down as they revolve. Overhead, strips of red and purple neon tubing line the ceiling. On the menu board above the place-your-order counter, and down below in the display cases where the doughnuts are laid out—the glazed and the jelly-filled and the old-fashioned and the sugared and the sprinkled and the chocolate-dipped—you see everything exactly as you would see it at a Mister Donut anywhere in the United States. Sometimes you can't get close to this counter. After school the place fills with kids standing in line for doughnuts and hot chocolate. At night, after dinner, adults sometimes suggest in all seriousness that you stop at Mister Donut for dessert. Why? For the rare taste of the doughnuts? No. Not entirely. Though a generation has now grown up with them as a feature of the urban landscape, these American doughnuts are still exotic.

On TV you see Joe Montana in his warm-up jacket speaking on behalf of SONY. In the video shop you see the posters for *Lethal Weapon, Two Jakes, Terminator II, Wall Street, Thelma and Louise*. Flying on Japan Airlines, you flip through the in-flight sales catalogue called *JAL-Shop*, which offers things to purchase in the air—jewelry, luggage, footwear, wristwatches. The ads are all in Japanese. The models are all Caucasian. Inside the Mister Donut at the northern end of Ohori Park in midtown Fukuoka, right next to the carousel where the mini-horses rise and turn, there is a jukebox, a Wurlitzer of the classic period, about four feet high, its top curved with neon tubing that shows no sign of age or discoloration. This is the real reason I stop here. It is the finest looking Wurlitzer I have seen in years.

The first time I walked through the door, the air was filled with the sound of the Chordettes singing "Mr. Sandman." I looked around the room, at the kids making a sweet-stop before heading home, at the young couple in their twenties having a late-day snack and rendezvous, splitting a large order of fries, at the father who had brought his two kids in for treats. He wore a down-filled windbreaker, just like the dads in the States. His kids, who looked to be around four and six, wore sweatshirts that said "Dallas Cowboys" and "UCLA."

I walked over to the Wurlitzer and flipped through the song cards. I found a solid list of hits from the '50s and '60s. The Platters doing "Only You." Richie Valens doing "La Bamba." Buddy Holly's "Peggy Sue." "I Get Around" by the Beach Boys. Chuck Berry. Fats Domino. Patsy Cline. All for 100 Yen a play, about seventy-five cents. Same price as the doughnuts. I stay away from the doughnuts. But I like the music. Sounds from home. I take my cup of coffee to a window seat, look out at the boulevard, and think about what swirls together in the days and nights of Fukuoka. Old-fashioned glazed. Sunday jogger. Kuroda clan. Toyota four-door. Torii gate. Shinto shrine. Border ballad. Computer chimes. Prosperity charms. Full-length mirror. Phone booth photos. The Chordettes harmonizing from 1954, still imploring that Sandman to bring them a dream and make him the cutest one they've ever seen . . .

COMING BACK

In the early days, almost all Japanese who immigrated to Hawai'i and the United States came from five or six southern prefectures such as this one, rural regions that were in deep economic trouble. Jeanne's father was among them. Now she has crossed the water in the opposite direction, to research a book about three generations of Japanese American women, and to make her first connection with her father's homeland.

That is what has brought us this far south. The fellowship lets us live anywhere we choose. From here it is easy to get out into the kind of countryside her parents and grandparents might have known, and it's a lot cheaper than Tokyo, where they say fifteen hundred dollars a month for a two-and-a-half-room apartment is not unusual. In Ropponmatsu five hundred dollars is getting us a studio with a stove and a fridge and a toaster oven and a western toilet and a shower stall with flex hose and two tables and a regular bed.

Shimazawa-san, the fastidious manager, speaks no English. So we bow a lot, walking in and out of the building, precede every request or overture with *"sumi-ma-sen"* ("Please forgive me for so boldly intruding upon your time and space"). It is one of about ten phrases I have now mastered (*Keko-des.* "It's okay." *Kom-ban-wah.* "Good afternoon"). Jeanne knows a lot more. Before we left, she took an eight-week crash course at the UC Santa Cruz Summer Language Institute. She surprised everyone, including herself.

For years she has claimed she knew nothing at all about spoken Japanese. But as we have settled into this neighborhood, I see how much she has carried in her bones and in her nerve-ends. While she was growing up her grandmother was still alive, puttering around the house, never speaking anything but the dialect she brought with her from her early years in Niigata. This in itself will leave its imprint for a lifetime. Jeanne can read the body language. She has an inner ear for the music of the words. Sometimes intonation tells her what the subject is likely to be—good news, bad news, the weather, an ailment, a compliment, an apology.

In the world of her extended family, now spread all up and down the California coast—the offspring of ten brothers and sisters, dozens of nieces and nephews with their dozens of spouses and countless relatives—certain words and phrases have lived on in the daily conversation. The names of foods and vegetables. Insults. Endearments. The names of cities and counties in Japan. At home in San Jose, ninety years after Jeanne's father left Japan, they still call chopsticks *hashi,* and rice *gohan* and soy sauce *shoyu,* and the New Year's Day dinner *shogatsu,* and when someone's legs are thick from the knees downward, that person is likely to be kidded about *daikon-ashi* (calves shaped like the thick and straight Japanese turnip).

HUMILITY

The day we moved in we brought a gift for Shimazawa-san and left it at the front desk. *Omiagi,* it is called, the endless passing back and forth of gifts to mark every occasion, large and small. The next morning, just before noon, his wife appeared at our door with a tray of food, a light lunch, a gesture of welcome: four large, round dumplings stuffed with spicy meat.

Jeanne and the wife of Shimazawa-san begin to talk, half in Japanese, half in English, which she once studied at the university. With Jeanne here, the wife suggests, perhaps she can practice her English on a regular basis. When Jeanne tells her she already speaks very well, the left hand flies up to her face, waving back and forth as if insects have attacked her.

"No no no no no, my Engrish very bad."

Whether the English is good or bad is not the point, of course. We will see this gesture repeatedly, everywhere we go, the head inclining, the hand brushing past the face, the frantic wave of denial, waving away every kind of compliment.

"No no no no no, my English no good."

"No no no no no, the food too cold."

"No no no no no, my son should try harder in school."

SANDBATH
RESURRECTION

We can both get some work done here, and this place is only two blocks from a market district with its bakery, rice shop, flower shop, vegetable stalls, a Superette where they carry coffee (beans, grounds, or instant), kimchee, Kellogg's Rice Flakes, bottled water, yogurt. Just what we've been looking for. But it took a while to get here. This is the downside of a fellowship with no strings attached and no living quarters assigned to you. It took a while to find our way to Ropponmatsu and wind our way up the narrow street bordered with concrete retaining walls to the compound we now call home.

Jeanne's grant is administered out of the International House in Tokyo. We spent the first three days there, coming down from jet lag, figuring out the money and the telephone, making calls, and trying to get our bearings. We had a few leads, of course, and we had Japan Rail passes, prepurchased tickets that gave us two weeks of discounted travel anywhere in the country. With these we spent two weeks house hunting by train, heading as far north as Yamagata, then back to Tokyo, then south from there by bullet train through the industrial corridor, Yokohama, Osaka, stopping in Fukuoka the first time only to change trains, for the slow local out to Sasebo, on the coast.

In California a friend gave us the address of a relative whose mother runs an inn, a *ryokan* in Sasebo, where there might be a rental unit close to the sea.

But one look told us this was not what we had in mind—a navy town, with too many American sailors, and a main street that looks too much like Laguna Beach, a shoreline strip spaced with palms, where lanes of cars rumble along through a pale, hazy, lemony light.

We moved farther south, into Kumamoto province, where some other friends had friends. The midsize town of Yatsushiro lies about ten miles from Mount Unzen, which had exploded a year earlier, buried part of a village, and made world headlines. Before we set out to look at a couple of apartments in her neighborhood, I asked the wife of our host what it was like to be this close to a live volcano. She opened the sliding glass door that led to their small bonsai garden and drew one finger across the outer side of the glass. The finger came away black. With a wistful grin she said, *"Unzen."*

We decided to try the city of Kagoshima, where some of Jeanne's relatives had come from. It sits right next to Mount Sakurajima, another active volcano that steams all the time and frequently spills ashes on the city. Its gorgeous cone stands against the sky and dominates the region. On the day we stepped off the train, a tall plume was billowing from the top of Sakurajima. Gasses tinted the afternoon, making the late sun a brilliant tangerine. From the depot, old trolley tracks led downtown.

"What do you think?" I said to Jeanne.

"L.A. in the 1940s."

"You mean the light?"

"Plus the streetcars."

"Shall we check it out?"

"I've seen enough. That mountain makes me nervous."

Kagoshima is the southernmost city in Japan, and we had not planned to go beyond it. But somewhere in our travels another American had told us we should look at Ibusuki, down at the lower end of the last peninsula on the island of Kyushu. The town was small, this woman said, and cheap, and close to the water, and warm most of the year, which is something to think about as fall turns to winter. It was the kind of thing that happens when you are on your way from Point A to Point B and you meet someone on a subway platform who has just come back from Point X, a place you've never heard of or thought of visiting, but a few days later there you are, wandering into an un-known town for reasons that are still not entirely clear.

House hunting, we told ourselves, as we walked out of the depot, hailed a cab, and taxied over to a low-budget inn we'd found in the pamphlet that comes with the Rail Pass. House hunting, we said again the next morning—though each day now it was harder to fight down the growing sense of dis-location. By that time we had moved in and out of too many inns and hotels and cabs and train stations. The bags were getting heavier, and after two weeks on this gypsy path, the quest, the adventure, the challenge of Japan was wearing thin. This country was too strange, and perhaps more trouble than it was worth.

As I woke the next morning I was having the second thoughts, or third thoughts, that can grip you in the early days of a long trip, when you begin to fear the whole expedition may be a terrible mistake. Remembering all the loose ends and unfinished business I'd left behind, I woke in the predawn of Ibusuki thinking, "What's going on? A week ago we had never *heard* of this place. And what am I really *doing* over here seven time zones away from my phone and my desk and my work and my stuff, all my carefully assembled time and stuff?"

Well, as they often say, when you are ready for the answer, the question will appear. And the answer was about to present itself, there in the strangest of all the strange places we had seen.

In this land of the unexpected, Ibusuki is the farthest from what we had expected to find. It does not resemble any of the Japans you see promoted or publicized. There are no world-class shrines or gardens. You don't find Kabuki there or sumo wrestling or cherry trees in bloom. There is no fast-track urban life, no sidewalk multitude streaming toward the underground trains. It was October. The streets were almost empty—a few honeymooning couples, a few elderly retirees, a few off-season site-seers from China and Korea. In the yards around the houses we saw a lot of cactus, and bushes of red hibiscus. Palm trees lined the boulevards, royal palms, date palms, palms with the spiky leaves Hawaiians use to make *lauhala* matting. The latitude is more southerly than San Diego, in line with northern Baja. Later a fellow from Tokyo who has been to the US would tell us, with a condescending city smile, "That part of Kyushu is what you might call the Alabama of Japan."

At the southern end of the island, two long peninsulas, like two facing crab claws, form Kagoshima Bay. Ibusuki lies inside this bay, on the protected inner edge of the peninsula called Satsuma, with a view across still waters toward the worn-down cliffs of former craters, now green and razor edged, much like the cliffs that line the north shore of the island of Kaua'i. Maybe this in itself has prepared me to surrender, something about the Polynesian look of the volcanic landscape that shaped the glassy bay, the steeply eroded peaks, the palms, the blue water lapping porous lava rocks.

After a morning of halfhearted apartment pricing, we do what Japanese heat seekers travel hundreds of miles to do and stroll over to the bath house, where steam from subterranean springs comes percolating right up through the sand. For three hundred yen you get a locker and a clean *yukata,* a long robe, blue on white. You can't wear anything underneath, says the woman who takes the money. "All off. No underpants. Nothing."

Inside the locker room you strip and don the robe and feel the crisp, freshly ironed cotton on your skin. (Half an hour later it will be dark with sweat and with the fine black sand you carry back to the bath house where you'll drop it in a soggy heap with all the other spent yukata, then shower off the sand and soap down and shower again and slide into the *furo*—the tile-lined tub filled with mineral water piped from the springs—for the finishing work, the final polish.)

Outside the bath house door rubber thongs, *zori,* are piled in a heap, several dozen, of varying sizes. We each grab a couple of these and clop along the concrete walkway, looking out across the dark sand turned black by wetness. Steam curls from the low-tide flats, much as it rises from the vents and fissures in the floor of Kilauea Caldera on the Big Island of Hawai'i. An important difference is that here the bonneted women await you, shovels in hand, standing by their rows of shallow graves.

We stretch out in the sand, attended by these shovel-bearing women, and one leans in so close to me, her eyes gazing into mine with an intimacy so tender, so disarming, I have to relax. I have to surrender. She wraps the white towel around my head and gently pulls it snug beneath my chin. She does not speak. She steps back and throws the first shovelful across my shoulder, black and hot and wet enough that it does not spread. Each grain seems to lie where it lands, making weight against the skin. The next shovelful lands on my belly, the next on my hips. Soon she has me buried to my neck, the dark sand pressing along my body, and steam rising through the sand beneath me, from the hot springs. Only my head shows, one head in a row of towel-wrapped heads lined along the black sand beach.

She looks to be about sixty. She wears the clothes of a country woman dressed for field work, baggy blue trousers, white apron, blue bonnet. She laughed when she saw me coming, laughed at my height. She spoke to the other women, all dressed alike, all carrying long-handled shovels, and they all laughed as she trenched an extra foot of sand so I could stretch at full length and join the others staring at the sky.

Now she leans on her shovel, and I am breathing slowly under the weight of all the sand, while the heat cooks my neck, my legs, my back. The women move away to meet some new arrivals who have walked down from the bath house. I close my eyes. For the first time in two weeks I feel at ease, at rest. Why? Is it just the sand and the beach air and the heat of this outdoor Asian sauna? Something I'd been barely aware of is being steamed away, some deep anxiety is dissolving, floating upward with the whispers of the moisture and the heat. For the first time since we landed in Japan, I feel connected. But how? And why here?

I doze.

The lap-lap of tiny waves revives me. My nose revives me. Both together. Splashing surf and itching nose. I cannot scratch. My arms and hands are buried. My eyes begin to itch. My chin. My neck. Suddenly each second is a little test of the will. I can force my arms upward through the sand to scratch away at my face and eyes, but that would break the crust, break open the cocoon of heat, break the spell.

I concentrate on voices. Whose are they? From Jeanne, from other towel-surrounded heads along the beach I hear nothing but the occasional intake—*Sssssssssssss*—a stoic hissing through the teeth, a long exhale. The voices come from the women with the shovels. Softly they chatter, in words I can't comprehend, as they move the sand around, smoothing, preparing it. I listen while the minutes pass. I can't say how many minutes. Two. Or ten. I listen until my itching subsides, and the nearby scratch of a shovel digging—*chk . . . chk . . . chk . . .*—is a gentle drumbeat calling me back to life.

It is the same woman, in her blue cotton trousers, white apron to her knees. She is working right next to me, clearing another space. She glances my way. Again our eyes meet, just a glimpse, an instant, and here at last I find the touchpoint—after two weeks of dislocated gypsy roaming—a first point of entry into this unknown and foreign land.

It is not the town of Ibusuki that touches me. We'll be out of here and on our way tomorrow afternoon. The touchpoint is located somewhere else. It is in the dark sand. It is inside the earth and the steam. It is in the eyes of this unnamed woman gazing out from under the brim of her white, farm-country bonnet. Sweat is pouring off my face, into the towel. I am cooking in my sweat, inside the wet cotton skin of my yukata. My back is stinging with the slow burn of steady heat you know is going to be good for you. And what comes rising through me, along with the heat, is a liberating form of knowledge, or perhaps memory—that the land is not foreign. It is familiar. This is the sand and the steam and the subsoil and the hot spring and the mountain peninsula of the globe we all inhabit. And the look in the eyes of this woman is familiar too. You would recognize it anywhere. She is the tender-eyed lover, and the mother tucking you in at night, and the one who has come to bury you so that you can be born again.

THE GLOBAL SOUNDTRACK

Afterward in the lobby we push some coins into the soft drink machine and carry the cans of cola outside to slake our thirst on the seawall of mortared lava. We watch the tide move in, slithering across the gray-black flats. Nearby, some Korean tourists are lining up to have a picture taken against the backdrop of the mirror bay and the razor peaks along its farther shore.

The air is filled with the sliding call of a steel guitar, coming from speakers mounted near the roof of the famous bath house at the southern end of Kyushu. Drifting out across the waters of Kagoshima Bay the song is "Only You and Blue Hawai'i." Followed by "The Hawaiian War Chant." Then "Lovely Hula Hands."

FIFTY YEARS
LATER

"Sumi-ma-sen," Jeanne says, whenever she has to introduce herself. *"Nihongo-wakari-ma-sen."* ("Please forgive me. I don't know Japanese.") *"America-jin-desu. Nisei desu. . . ."* ("I am an American, second generation. But my father was born in Hiroshima prefecture. He moved to America in 1904. All his life he dreamed of returning to Japan. I am the youngest of his ten children, and I am here to complete the journey he always wanted to make.")

It is a brief yet powerfully effective speech, opening little doors of recognition everywhere—the daughter's sense of loyalty, suitably couched in self-effacement, a trait the Japanese much admire. And the name *Hiroshima* carries such a heavy charge that nothing needs to be said in words, or can be said.

The head of the listener will incline in a quick nod, while the face and eyes say, Yes, we know that place, it is within reach, just a hundred miles or so to the north, and yes, we know what it means if you have had family ties to that region, and yes, even though your father, for whatever reason, chose to leave his homeland behind, he himself was spared the horror of what happened there in 1945, and that surely has to be a blessing.

Her father was spared, and yet he was not spared. He had become a man without a country. When World War II began he had been a resident of the US for almost forty years, but he still was not a citizen, since in those days immigrants from Asia weren't allowed to naturalize. He had liked America. He preferred it to Japan and often said so. He wanted to naturalize. He couldn't. Bureau of Immigration policy prevented it.

All his children were US citizens. His wife was a citizen because she'd been born on the Hawaiian island of Kaua'i where Jeanne's Japanese grandparents had come as plantation hands, working off a labor contract. By the time the war began, Jeanne's father had spent two-thirds of his very full life on the West Coast, yet he was still classified as an "enemy alien."

They were all regarded as enemies then, including Jeanne, born in Inglewood, pulled out of the third grade at age eight, loaded onto a bus in downtown L.A. and ferried a day's bus ride north, across the Mojave Desert, to Manzanar. She and her family spent the three wartime years inside a barbed wire compound with ten thousand others of Japanese ancestry, most of them American citizens—and there were nine other camps like Manzanar.

That was a half a century ago, of course, and you keep telling yourself it's a different world now. Fifty years later she has landed a generous grant to spend six months traveling and writing, a grant jointly funded by Japan and the United States. She is one of six Americans over here this year pursuing their creative work, while six Japanese are somewhere in the States. The long-range goal: to broaden understanding from one culture to another.

And yet . . . and yet . . . those old and contradictory attitudes are in the air again. Jeanne feels them even here, seven thousand miles across the water. The Pearl Harbor anniversary has had a lot to do with this. Old wounds have been reopened. New wounds are being rediagnosed, or reimagined. We get letters from friends in Los Angeles who tell us how the Southeast Japanese Community Center in Norwalk was hit by vandals. The walls were spray painted "Go Back to Asia." Not long ago in Sacramento the home of a Japanese American couple was firebombed. Visitors from Tokyo have been shot at in Walnut Creek outside the BART station, and on the streets of San Francisco. In San Jose, before we left, I saw a sleek-looking delivery van with this bumper sticker:

SCREW JAPAN
Courtesy of Allied Auto Parts

I think it is all connected. Spray paint and immigration and economics and the fifty-year-old spectre of World War II. And the exchange of capital between corporate America and corporate Japan. And the efforts of certain CEOs and talk-show hosts and congressmen and novelists to recast the Japanese as the villains in a transpacific melodrama.

What troubles us is the way corporate dealing is so often used to feed the negative view of an entire nation, and then—via the ethnic ripple effect—a negative view of all those long-gone and distant relatives who now inhabit various parts of the United States.

The spray paint in Norwalk. The firebomb in Sacramento. The contests in Detroit to smash apart a Datsun with sledgehammers. For Jeanne these are like notes ringing in the wind, high-pitched notes that can drift all the way across the ocean on the same wind that used to blow through the Owens Valley back in 1942, through the barbed wire fencing around the internment camp where she spent her childhood with all her American-born brothers and sisters because their background happened to be Asian.

A NEW
METAPHOR

En route we stopped in Honolulu. The anniversary was still weeks away, but no one could talk about anything else. The place was crackling with anticipation. Hotels had been sold out for months in advance. Elderly veterans and their wives were already in town. You would see them strolling along Kalakaua Avenue in matching overseas caps and sateen jackets that featured the names of their hometowns and their wartime units. Often they would be outnumbered by clusters of young honeymooners from Tokyo and Nagasaki in matching aloha shirts.

Everyone was asking, "Who won the war?"

It struck us as an odd question, considering that the war they referred to had ended so long ago. The world we inhabit now scarcely resembles the world back then. But in the air above the Pacific this question lingers on. You hear it in Honolulu and in Los Angeles and in Pebble Beach.

You don't hear it in Fukuoka. For the Japanese the war ended with the bombing of Hiroshima. They lost. And they know it. They lost their cities, their military, their resources, their honor, and their pride. They lost everything, and they started over from ground zero, with enormous aid from the United States. In recent years, as Japan's fortunes rise and fall, they sometimes seem to be winning something else. And somewhere in the American imagination, whatever is being won is all too often perceived as another campaign in the war that began in 1941.

In Hawai'i they have a particularly hard time thinking about the Japanese. They can't live with them, and they can't live without them. Most of the hotels now are Japanese owned. There was a rising complaint, throughout the 1980s, about a systematic takeover of the islands. High purchase prices were driving up the costs of land and housing. Fewer and fewer islanders could afford to buy homes in their homeland. Then the buying spree began to slow. Maybe it was over. Then tourism dropped off, in the year after the Persian Gulf crisis, when threats of terrorism loomed over every international airport. Before long a trade delegation from Hawai'i had flown to Tokyo, led by Governor John Waihe'e. Their message, in brief, "Please don't go away."

At a Waikiki restaurant one night I was talking with a woman who has lived in Hawai'i for a number of years, a woman I think of as warm spirited and well connected. She was describing the many preparations for the fiftieth. Ceremonies would be held on the deck of the U.S.S. *Missouri*. Heroes would be gathering, thousands of vets. Senators would be flying in, generals, admirals, maybe the president. No foreign dignitaries had been invited. They had definitely decided against that. Everyone knew "foreign" meant Japanese.

"Too bad," I said, "considering all the international tension in the air just now. It could be a golden opportunity for some public forgiveness, visibly and officially leaving the war behind and the scars of war, clearing the way . . ."

"Oh no, not necessarily," she said. "There is a lot of local feeling that they should make some gesture of apology for doing what they did and for starting the Pacific war. But you see, they have never done that."

"It's true. An apology is long overdue. But how about us? Have we ever apologized for the bombing of Hiroshima?"

"That's different."

"They say eighty thousand people died in the first two minutes. Mostly civilians."

"We only did that because they bombed us first. The feeling is that Pearl

Harbor was an act of aggression, and the Japanese still have not shown sufficient regret."

"But maybe we shared some of the responsibility there," I said. "We may have brought it on ourselves."

"What do you mean?"

"If we hadn't taken Hawai'i away from the Hawaiians back in 1893 and then turned it into a military arsenal, maybe there wouldn't have been anything to attack."

For a while she didn't speak.

"When we brought all our ships out here in the 1920s and '30s, maybe we created the target. Shouldn't we at least acknowledge this?"

Others had been listening. Now a silence had fallen over the till-then animated table. Everyone was looking at me.

"If we're really interested in apologies and forgiveness," I said, "maybe the place to begin would be for us to apologize to the Hawaiians for overthrowing their government by force and then transforming these islands into such a dangerous place."[2]

It was the wrong thing to say. It ended the conversation. Nobody wanted to talk about that. They wanted to talk about the presidential entourage and the impact this would have on local traffic and hotel security, and I was not surprised. It is human nature to shove your own misdeeds under the rug of history and keep the finger of blame pointed outward.

I don't mean to say that the Japanese military should be excused. A sneak attack is a sneak attack. They did terrible things during World War II.

But what about us? Are our hands clean? All of military history is filled with atrocities, ours included. The atomic bombings of Hiroshima and Nagasaki were grievous crimes, as are so many acts of war. Yet there is still a place in our national memory that makes them allowable, somehow forgivable, acts we aren't obliged to feel apologetic about. Meanwhile, when the subject is Pearl Harbor, we will overlook our own misdeeds and let our indignation be fed by what the Japanese did half a century ago—or rather, by what certain generals and admirals decided to do.

I keep running into people who would like to blame all Japanese, and sometimes, by association, or by osmosis, anyone else of Asian background, for everything that has happened from 1941 onward—as if decisions by generals and admirals and captains of industry always represent the national will, or the ethnic will.

Last week I met a woman whose mother marched through the streets of Tokyo in 1941, among a multitude of women who had passionately opposed and protested that war. Thousands of women marched, she told me, risking their lives by taking a public stand against the powers of the day, willing to because they were appalled by what the generals were doing to their country.

I recently talked with a man who was evacuated from Tokyo early in 1945, just before the capitol was firebombed and flattened by our B-29s. He was eight at the time, one among thousands of kids sent out to camps in the countryside, living on handfuls of rice, watching their bellies swell with malnutrition. "I remember when my stomach first started sticking out," he said, "I thought it was a good sign. I had had almost nothing to eat for many days, but my belly seemed to be saying it was full."

Suppose everyone apologized to everyone? Wouldn't that be a civilized place to begin a new level of dialogue? Haven't we held too tightly to this long-ago attack? It has become a cherished metaphor, telling us over and over again what we have wanted to believe. Fifty years go by, but the metaphor burns on and on. Why is it that so many accounts of our economic difficulties have included references to Pearl Harbor? How often do you hear references to Japan's decision to close its doors to the west, back in the seventeenth century, or to any other event in their two-thousand-year history? Do Japan bashers ever cite the arrival of Commodore Perry's fleet in Tokyo Bay in 1853, pressuring the shogunate to open the country's ports to western trade?

The event we have preferred to emphasize is the sneak attack, since it seems to tell us the most about the people across the water. It tells us how the Japanese do things: they sneak up on you when you aren't looking. It tells us what we wish were true about ourselves: we have been the unwitting and unwilling victims of a wrongful and shameful assault upon our otherwise efficient, responsible, well-intentioned system of government and finance.

As a moment in history, Pearl Harbor was a crucial turning point. As a military event, it should never be forgotten. As a metaphor, it has outlived its usefulness, distorting our perceptions of the Japanese.

ᘇ

Maybe we could use a new metaphor.

ᘇ

Maybe it could be the sport of sumo wrestling. You see a lot of that here. There is something naked and pure about sumo. It is pure impact. Nothing can be concealed. The wrestlers crouch, their eyes only a few inches apart. They wear no uniforms. No gloves. No helmets. No shoes. And in sumo there are no weight divisions. It is not like boxing, where heavy goes against heavy, and welter meets welter. Wrestlers are known, of course, for their thickness and the body bulk cultivated by large meals followed by long afternoon naps. But speed counts too. Reflexes. Psychological readiness. There is a tradition of prolonged eye contact, before the lunge, as you gauge the will and courage of your opponent.

THE NATIONAL
PASTIME

In Fukuoka the wrestlers come to town each fall and stay for a month or so. It's a great source of local pride, since this is one of only three cities outside Tokyo where major tournaments are held. Nationwide there are six each year, three in the capitol, one in Osaka, one in Nagoya, and one right here. Early in November a team started working out at a shrine about a mile from where we live, so we had the lucky chance to watch some champions at very close range.

Sumo has a lot in common with the interior line. Maybe it is a Japanese equivalent of football, but with a longer and more elaborate history. The action is much like what goes on play after play, when the bulky running guard hurls himself at the massive defensive tackle, two huge men conditioned by diet and by training to do this very thing—to crouch, to lunge, to meet shoulder to shoulder and chest to chest, until one disposes of the other. In the swirl of play it is a burst of energy we often miss, while our TV-guided eyes follow the ball or the fate of the quarterback. Sumo takes that brief collision, male on male, skin to skin—no shirts, no pads, no face-guards—and makes of it the main event, the ultimate ritual, the national pastime.

In town for the big November tournament, they work out every morning, starting early, the novices first, with the celebrities showing up around 8:30 or 9 AM. Then they all break for a lunch that would last most of us a week, and roll over like hibernating grizzlies to sleep.

Our guide is Thad Nodine, who has become a sumo aficionado. He did graduate work at UC Santa Cruz and has a two-year job teaching English here at Seinan University. He's a lean and amiable fellow, wearing a coat and tie for the class he has to meet later on, wheeling his bike, telling us some of the workouts are closed to the public, but at this particular shrine it's okay to hang around and watch the action.

Behind Tojin marketplace we pass through a torii gate and into the garden, a space between apartment high-rises where dwarf pines are dark green in the morning sun. The shrine is old and steep-roofed and made of wood, the altar dimly visible within. Shinto reaches back to more rural and earthier times, when key moments in the planting year were ritualized. When the rice crops were going in, there would be celebrations both religious and festive. The many animal and earthly deities were to be respected, but they also liked to be entertained. For centuries wrestling played a part in these observances. To this day, handfuls of rice are used to purify the ring before a match begins, and wrestlers will be found working out on temple grounds.

Across the garden from the shrine, one wall of a low square building is covered with canvas. We peel back a corner and step into a room full of nearly naked men. A dozen other spectators are lined along the wall. A couple of them carry cameras. The floor is dirt. In the center is the ring, fifteen feet across, made of thick rope half-buried, tied with loops of twine. Inside this circle, which can never be touched by anything but the bare foot, and which can never be entered by a female, two men are crouched, facing each other across two short white lines fixed in the dirt like twin pitcher's mounds.

They're breathing hard. They have been at it for a while. They are waiting, breathing and waiting, their eyes locked. Each one wears a thick belt around his waist, tied in back, with a strap looping through the crotch. One belt is black, one is white. White is the higher rank. The fellow wearing the white belt looks small for a sumo wrestler. Thad tells me he is the smallest white belt in Japan, and highly regarded.

Small does not mean thin or tiny. He probably weighs two hundred pounds. His belly is round and smooth, but not vast. His legs look formidable. His skin all over is smooth and not particularly muscular in appearance.

That is, he has not lifted weights in order to create the high bicep definition and sharp pec line Americans associate with "a build." You can't see his triceps or his trapezius. But when these two finally crouch, by some mutual sign that is never voiced—perhaps a glance across the line, by which each man knows the moment is *now*—when they crouch, with feet wide apart and hands hanging close to the dirt, then lunge and meet in midair with the loud slap of flesh on flesh, and the legs planted behind like posts slanted to absorb great pressure—you can see that whatever this white belt lacks in weight he makes up for in some kind of alpha male, elephant bull reserve of channeled power.

The black belt outweighs him by around fifty pounds. Pushing chest to chest they grapple for handholds on the thick waistbands. The black belt is losing ground. One foot slides, tries to brace against the ring. Then he is upright and falling back, a foot lands outside the ring, and that's it. Step outside the ring, or let any part of your body but your foot touch the dirt, you lose the match. The black belt moves back, and another fellow moves forward, another black belt eager to test himself.

In this room there are twenty wrestlers practicing for the tournament that starts in ten days. Thad comments on our luck, our extraordinary timing. All the major wrestlers in Japan are practicing like this, at shrine sites around the city. The group we've come to watch, Thad calls it this "stable," includes four men from Hawai'i, two young black belts and two famous white belts— Akebono (Chad Rowan), the tallest of the big-time wrestlers, at six foot eight, and Konishiki, the American-born Samoan. In this stable he is currently an *ozeki,* thus the last to arrive.

When he finally pushes past the canvas flap and comes swaying into the arena, Konishiki seems to occupy about one-fourth of the total space. He unties his sash and removes his tent-size yukata. Gobs of flesh keep his immense legs spread, so that he both sways and waddles. Gobs hang from his upper arms, melons of excess. His belly is the largest I have ever seen. It seems to have a life of its own, a heaving dome strapped to his torso, for clearing the way as he moves. His calves are the size of punching bags. His black hair is pulled up into a knot on top of his head and tied with white string.

Konishiki is breathing heavily, just from the effort of transporting his weight across the room to the ring, which he now occupies, waiting for Akebono to join him. They are sparring partners, and Thad says it's a rare treat to see these two high-ranked wrestler/stars working out together. You seldom wrestle publicly against a stable-mate. Thus far they have never met like this in competition.

Today Akebono can't seem to move him. At 450 or so he is still outweighed by 100 pounds, and at six foot eight he can't get close enough to the ground to come in from underneath. Round after round the big Samoan, barrel legs planted, drives Akebono out of the ring, forces him back toward the rim. After each round Konishiki seems ready to expire from the task and from lack of breath. The great chest heaves. Pain crosses his dark and otherwise lineless Polynesian face (he is twenty-seven). He turns and sways toward an open window and leans on the sill to take in some outside air. Meanwhile, younger wrestlers attend to him, towel the sweat off his back, wipe sand from his legs, hand him a cup of water. He doesn't ask for this attention. He doesn't speak to them, or look at them, or acknowledge them much. He is their top man, their *ozeki*. They are the admiring apprentices.

Though he never quite gets his breath, eventually he sways back to the ring and squats low. He looks at Akebono, looks away. Akebono stands up, towering over everyone, goes to get another drink, comes back to the line, squats and waits. At last they are ready. No one signals or rings a bell or calls "Go." They know when to move. In the same instant they lunge, one thousand pounds of flesh collide, chest to chest, shoulder to shoulder, the open hands shoving for advantage, reaching for the waist, for the hold. Their faces are contorted. Their legs are pillars. For several seconds they are suspended there, and maybe this round Akebono has the advantage . . .

※

At 560 pounds Konishiki is the heaviest champion in the history of sumo. You might think all he has to do is stand there, an immovable monument of flesh and bone. Not so. In the midst of the high ritual that surrounds this sport, sumo is full of surprises. Two weeks later he will win the tournament here, but only after one match, short but significant, that astounds everyone, most of all Konishiki himself.

He was up against a much lighter man, a young favorite on the rise through the carefully controlled hierarchy of rankings. This fellow weighed in at about 265. Next to the huge Samoan he seemed wizened and underfed. When they crouched in the sandy ring, surrounded by thousands of animated fans, it was almost ludicrous, a sumo satire. But an odd thing happened.

So much of Konishiki's weight is in his belly that when he walks he has to lean his shoulders back and keep his feet wide to maintain balance. In the ring, as he crouches, his belly looms in front of him. What the smaller man did was plunge straight into this belly, head low. Unable to see over the mountain of his own girth, Konishiki tried to reach across the other fellow's back and get a handhold on the broad waistband. To do this he had to raise up, lifting slightly, thus losing his center of gravity. In that instant the lighter man, still lunging, shoved him right out of the ring to win the match in fifteen seconds. Lucky for Konishiki this happened early in the tournament. He was stunned, perhaps stunned out of an overreliance on his own enormous and unwieldy bulk.

OTHER
WARRIORS

The wrestlers retire to the dining room to put away their daily ration of rice and the hearty stew called *chanko nabe,* thick with vegetables, fish, meat, and chicken. Jeanne and I walk back across Ohori Park. The wrestling has stirred up memories of her older brother, Woody. "He would have enjoyed this a lot," she says. "He used to do a great sumo imitation when we were kids."

Woody had been the family comedian. Named for Woodrow Wilson, he was short and stout, much like some of the men we'd just seen. But he had been a combatant of a different sort. In the lean years after World War II he had worked the professional wrestling circuit for a while, with a fellow who went by the name of Mister Moto. In that nightly melodrama, then as now, you had the good guys and the bad guys. Woody and Mister Moto had their roles cut out for them. They were the Devious Orientals.

It was a strange fate for a man who, just a few years earlier, had served as a translator and special agent with US Army Intelligence. While the rest of the family was still interned behind the fences at Manzanar, Woody had enlisted and was sent to the South Pacific, during the years of the thickest fighting. He interrogated captured Japanese soldiers. He monitored short-wave messages. After the truce was signed, in August 1945, he was among the first Americans to enter postwar Japan.

From Tokyo he made a pilgrimage south to the village called Kake, outside Hiroshima, and looked up an old great-aunt who had known and loved his father. By that time she was in her eighties. Woody saw the country house that had been stripped by war, stripped of furniture and fittings and food. In this old woman's eyes he saw his father, and he wondered how his own life might have turned out if she had not come up with the money that had allowed her favorite nephew to leave the village and cross the ocean.

Back in California, after discharge, Woody and his brothers tried to revive the family business. As an "enemy alien," his father had lost his commercial fishing license. For years the state would not renew it. The family's boats had been confiscated and never returned. The man without a country was temporarily the father without a job. As a citizen and veteran, Woody could get a license and a loan. With another brother he could lease a boat. But the hours were long and the money wasn't very good, and he now had a wife and children to support. When the opportunity came his way to make quite a bit more for a lot less work, he took it. He teamed up with Mister Moto, calling himself Suki (half of Wakatsuki, the family name).

He cultivated a chin beard. He donned yukata and samurai sash. As Mister Moto's faithful valet, he would play at being treacherous. He would prowl around the edges of the ring, waiting to sneak a karate chop through the ropes. The crowd would boo and hiss, and he would put on his most inscrutable smile. Mister Suki. A poor man's Fu Manchu. The Yellow Peril as ringside theatre.

Jeanne remembers that offstage, at home in Long Beach, he could get the whole family laughing, as he made the face that would amuse the crowd, or sometimes ignite their anger and their outcries.

"Sometimes," Jeanne says, "they would actually throw things. But Woody would say, Hey, it's steady work, and I get to travel, and Moto and me we're laughing all the way to the safe deposit box."

IN THE
STEAMING
WORLD

Jeanne's earliest memories are full of steam rising from tubs of water. Before he started fishing, her father had farmed for several years in southern California. Next to the field there was a shed, a metal roof held up by four corner posts. Under the roof there was a large wooden tub with metal flooring, and under the tub a fire pit. There were benches to sit on, and boards over the metal to protect the feet. This was where they would sometimes gather in the early evening after work. She remembers the soft voices, the ecstatic groans as they sat immersed in the heat and the steam, her mother and father, older sisters and brothers.

At home in Santa Cruz we have a hot tub sitting out next to the fence, with a gas heater and an electric pump, and we use it a lot. But Japan's steam, for Jeanne, is in a different category. This is ancestral steam, percolating upward for millennia. When she enters it, she too is somehow transformed, or heated in some other way, an older way that is, for her, a new way.

It's another reason Kyushu is the right place for us to be located. Island of craters, some live, some dormant. Island of hot springs, some public, some private.

Between Christmas and New Year's we travel across the island to the town of Yufuin, at the northern edge of a national park that stretches from Mount

Aso—site of the world's largest volcanic caldera—to Beppu Bay. The town is laid out inside an embracing half-moon of mountains, with Mount Yufuin the topmost peak, rising through misty clouds, the kind of cloud-and-mountain vista you have been led to expect from Japan, if you have dwelled on the Hokusai woodcuts or Kurosawa's films.

Thanks to a Japanese friend in Fukuoka we are staying at a *ryokan* where there have never been any American guests. It is a little private park inside the town, with sculpted shrubs around a lawn half green, half wintry brown. Hot water trickles from a standpipe into a stone bowl, sending steam across the grass. The low roofs are tiled with slate. With the mist-surrounded mountains for a backdrop, it has the Japanese-y look you have hoped would still be available *some*where.

Our contact, a bilingual woman who works with the US Information Service, calls this a "Union Mansion," an inn built for and most often used by employees of a manufacturer of running shoes and sporting supplies. Once before, she told us, she had arranged for some Americans to stay here, but they had left behind a very bad feeling.

"What happened?" we asked.

"They were on a lecture tour," she told us, "and they had been spending all their time in the big cities. They wanted to get out to the countryside and see 'the real Japan.' So I made the arrangements, helped with the train tickets, gave them the address. They took a taxi from the depot and came into the compound there. The manager showed them to the building. Their room was the second one along the hall. They did not take off their shoes. They stepped into the hallway and opened the door and stepped up onto the tatami mat with their shoes on and took one look at the room. I suppose it was too small, or perhaps looked too bare. The futon and blankets, of course, were all stacked behind the screen, which was closed. They walked back out to the street without saying a word to the manager about their intentions, and so he assumed they would be returning.

"He had to keep the room available overnight, and eventually we had to pay him for that, plus the food that he had set aside. It was very embarrassing. I assured him that you were not going to be that way, so he must not worry. He will be very pleased to see you. Of course, this is why I had to ask you for the payment in advance."

With the national reputation at stake, we are on our best behavior as we step past the gateway of polished logs and into the courtyard. Bowing to the elderly manager, we introduce ourselves.

"*Sumi-ma-sen . . .*" ("Please forgive us. We are the Americans from Fukuoka . . .")

He is cordial, bowing, spry, and wrinkled, five feet tall or so. In Japanese he tells us that he has never been to Fukuoka, though he has heard it is a very fine city—speaking of this regional metropolis that lies two hours west as if we have just arrived from someplace as curious and remote as Calcutta or London.

We follow him across the compound to an entry door, where we bow again, and thank him again, humbly, profusely.

"*Arigato. Arigato go-zai-mas.*"

From our shoes we step into slippers, choosing pairs from the many slippers of various sizes lined up just inside the door. We walk four paces along the short hallway to another door, which opens onto a narrow standing space, where we leave the slippers in order to step up, with stocking feet, onto the tightly woven matting.

No doubt about it, this room is spartan, or rather, stripped down to the essentials, in the classic Japanese manner. No chairs. No TV. No magazines. On one side, shoji screens slide back to reveal a view across the gardens, toward the bath house. The tatami mat is bordered with fine brocade. There is a lacquered table close to the floor, with tea service waiting, bowls, saucers, small teapot, and canister of tea.

Everything here is close to the floor, and the ceilings are low, and there is no mystery about why the Japanese have such a high respect for their spaces, a respect that is signaled by the efficiency of so many small moves and gestures. In these small and carefully arranged rooms there is little margin for error. Particularly for someone my size—six foot two—any large or sudden move is going to knock something over or send you crashing through the paper screen.

In the closet, freshly ironed robes and sashes are waiting on hangers. We climb out of our western clothes, put on the robes—kimono for women, yukata for men—and step down into our slippers, to slide along to the end of the hallway, where we step from the slippers into the wooden clogs you use to go clopping along the path of fitted stones to the bath house, a wood-frame changing room that leads you to the baths, the *on-sen*.

The pools are outdoor/indoor, half covered, half open to the sky, fed from nearby springs and lined with mortared river stones. Shrubbery comes right up to the pool, shrubs trimmed to make domes and curving bubbles of foliage. Above the shrubs dwarf sugar pines are trimmed to make wheels of brushy limb-work puffing out around the shortened trunks. The trees and plants are interspersed with chunks of lava rock, black, or iron red.

In the pools it is intensely quiet. The ryokan is bounded on two sides by rows of houses and the narrow streets of Yufuin, yet it is enclosed and encased in a globe of silence, and inside the globe the trickle of water steaming from its bamboo spout somehow punctuates the stillness, making a little sound-sculpture inside this busy, busy land where a hundred and twenty-five million people are crammed together within a space slightly smaller than the state of California.

❧

We are traveling this time with Jane Yamashiro, a longtime ally from Honolulu, who happens to be on her way to Okinawa, four hundred miles south of here. Jane was born in Hawai'i, grew up on the Big Island, where her family farmed. Now she works for the university as a specialist in community outreach. She had some vacation time coming, so she has combined that with the Holidays for a trip back to the home island her grandparents left nearly a hundred years ago.

She and Jeanne could almost be sisters. They are about the same height, five foot three. They have the same kind of sunny smile and ready laugh, and between them there is a strong and sisterly bond. And yet their features are not the same. Jane has a distinctly Okinawan look. Her hair is naturally curly. Her eyes are somewhat rounder than Jeanne's, her skin a shade darker, her face a bit broader. Her name too is region specific. Everyone named Yamashiro, she says, can trace their family back to Okinawa.

She has been to Japan before and has been studying the language for years. Talking with the manager, she has already started to break the code on the local dialect. When we return from the baths in a mood to eat, she can click on the intercom and speak into the tiny microphone set discreetly next to the doorjamb and tell the old man and his wife we are ready for dinner.

It arrives on large lacquered trays—sashimi with shredded radish, shrimp tempura, salty dried fish, shredded cabbage, and the pickled bits of cabbage called *tsukemono,* white rice, green tea, and custard-yellow egg-cup, very salty, garnished with one more piece of fish.

There's plenty, more than we can finish. We spread it out across the low table and sit cross-legged, taking our time, picking our way with chopsticks, talking as the sky outside turns from dusk to early dark. Later we go to the baths again, then open out the futons and spread them across the matting and turn in early, loose, boiled to drowsiness, skin humming with the heat.

What I remember most vividly from this excursion is a scene the next morning, though not really a scene—a moment, a glimpse back into an earlier time. We were all up with the first light for a prebreakfast soak, and at that hour we had the place to ourselves. We had seen one other party on the grounds, a younger couple, and they were sleeping in. So there we were, clopping along, breathing puffs of fog. I was in the lead and turned to look back just as Jeanne and Jane came around the corner of the building and stepped out onto the path of stones.

Each of them wore the blue-and-white kimono, sashed at the waist, and *getas,* the high-rise wooden clogs. Jeanne's hair was knotted behind her head to keep it out of the water we would soon be wading into. Around them the sculpted shrubs, the dwarf pines of this self-contained little park; behind them the tiled roof of the inn, tinted silver, and a misty swirl at the top of Mount Yufuin, which rose in silhouette against a silvery dawn.

These two women from across the sea, one from California, one from Hawai'i, had suddenly stepped back a hundred years or so. They became, for just an instant, the kind of women Jeanne was here to seek out and research and somehow get to know: the *Meiji-no-onna,* women of the era when her grandmother was a girl, up early for a hot bath in the springs bubbling outside some backcountry village and years before anyone she knew had ever thought of heading for America.

THE BATH
HOUSE AT
FUTSUKAICHI

New Year's. Jane is still in town. We have been out on a temple trip, site-seeing, heading back to the city, when we recognize a name on the station wall and make a last-second decision to hop off and try the baths for which this town is famous. Futsukaichi is a suburb of Fukuoka, right on the train line, a few miles due south. There are springs under the town, which means many bath houses to choose from.

We pick a place called *Baden Haus*. Except for the name, there is nothing German about it. Until we walk through the door, it does not occur to us that this is New Year's Eve. Baden Haus is a public bath, and the place is packed with local Japanese coming in for the ritual year-end purification and cleansing.

You pay 365 yen, about three dollars, and leave your shoes in the lobby by the soft-drink machines. It's segregated bathing, men on one side, women on the other. In slippers of molded green rubber you slide into the locker room and leave your clothes in one of the coin-operated metal lockers. From there you walk into a gym-size room rolling with steam, so that you are sweating as soon as you step through the high glass double doors. Before you enter the tubs you have to soap down.

Since all the faucets are taken, I have to wait a while. There are sixteen faucets, in two rows, with shower hoses attached. In front of each faucet a naked Japanese fellow sits squatting on one of the low plastic stools, scrubbing, soaping, washing his hair. One little kid about five years old is scrubbing his daddy's back. Then daddy gets up and puts the kid on the stool, and it is dad's turn to do the scrubbing.

I look around. I am the only *gaijin,* the only foreigner, probably four inches taller than the next tallest guy, but no one pays me any attention. That is, I don't *see* anyone paying me any attention, though they surely are. I can see a smaller room, glass-enclosed, a steamy cubicle open to the dark, wintry sky. And on an upper level there is a sauna with a cold plunge nearby. In this all-male room of steam and sweat some of the younger men are very modest and keep their genitals covered whenever they are out of the water. Even in the locker room they keep themselves covered. The towel you get is too small to tie around your waist, so they will hold the mini-towel next to the belly, to stay covered while walking from the glass doors to a tub, then lift the towel away just as they slide into the water.

Finally I have a faucet and squat down on an eight-inch-high stool to give myself a good soaping from head to foot. In the Japanese bathing tradition, cleanliness is not only next to godliness; it *is* godliness. Soaping down before the bath is like removing your shoes at the entrance to the ryokan and stepping into slippers, and then removing the slippers before you step up onto the tatami mat that covers the floor of your room. The dirt and grime of the outside world has been twice removed, and the tatami is a version of the cleanliness within that must be preserved.

I step into the largest tub, where water spills down a tiled wall, spreading into a foot-wide stream that makes a gliding, gleaming waterfall. A few other men are in there, sitting on submerged tile benches, just their heads showing, gazing past one another, gazing into the steam, soaking up the heat, not talking.

From this tub, water spills into the next one, where jacuzzi jets bubble. But I stay with the pool below the waterfall, the slow currents pouring over me, at 108 degrees or so, thinking this is a pretty civilized way to let the gone year steam and sweat itself into yesterday.

❦

Half an hour later I am in the lobby cooling off, sipping on a club soda and getting ready to head outside again where I know it is cold enough to snow. When Jeanne and Jane walk out into the lounge from the women's side, I see again what I glimpsed at Yufuin.

This time it has nothing to do with the clothes. There are no kimonos or getas or misty Kurosawa mountains in the background. They wear jeans and running shoes and thick socks and thick wool sweaters, and this waiting lounge at the Baden Haus in Futsukaichi with its foggy windows and crowded couches covered with old leatherette and aging soft-drink machines along the walls, this could be the Greyhound station in Albuquerque, New Mexico, in 1957.

This time, whatever the steam has done is showing in their eyes and in their faces. It is now 10 PM on New Year's Eve, and we have washed and soaked our way through the kind of ritual year-end purification that was traditional in Jeanne's family when she was growing up. But this time she happens to be in Japan. She and Jane have spent an hour in a room full of Japanese women, a room thick with steam and running water and shampooed hair and mothers with their daughters. Along with what the steam will always do for the body—polish the eyes, relax the skin, open the capillaries and all the invisible channels through which our fluids and ethers have to flow—some layer of cultural knowledge has been added, or reconfirmed, or reawakened. And they are joined again with their histories through the medium of steam that has been rising from these islands for so many hundreds and thousands of years.

HONESTY

To trigger a lock in the locker room at Baden Haus, you insert a 100-yen coin and turn the key. After the bath, you reinsert the key and retrieve your clothes, and you also get your coin back. It drops into a little cup below the lock. I didn't know this, so I didn't notice the coin there, and didn't think to look for it after I had dressed. I was heading for the lobby when a young fellow came running after me.

"*Go-men-a-sai,*" he said. ("I beg your pardon.") He looked about twenty-five. He had just come in and had started to use that same locker. He couldn't speak much English. His face was wide open, flushed, eager. "From your rocker," he said with an embarrassed smile, handing me the coin.

This morning in a supermarket down in the Tojin district, I passed a bulletin board on the wall nearest the cash registers, the kind of board used in the States for handwritten notices of cars for sale, apartments wanted. Among the various local notices on this board, there were two credit cards some shoppers had dropped or misplaced. They were just hanging there, attached with scotch tape, waiting for the owners to return.

At the higher echelons of cash flow, you have a level of treachery that has become part of the national legend. You have the notorious Yakuza, and a government continually shaken by scandalous stories of embezzlement and enormous bribes. But at the level of day-to-day transaction, you soon see that you can trust the people on the street, the clerks, the merchants. After cab rides you never have to count your change.

The day after we got back from Yufuin, Jane discovered that she had lost her camera. We tried to re-create the trip, and she was sure she'd had it when we climbed aboard the train back to the city. She must have left it on the seat. In most countries of the world you would have kissed that three-hundred-dollar piece of equipment good-bye. But she had been to Japan before and had lost things before. She decided to check with the Japan Rail downtown office and try the Lost and Found.

The fellow on duty wanted to know first the day of her trip, and then the number of her train and its time of arrival in Fukuoka, and then which car she had been sitting in. With that, he stepped into another room where Jane could see dozens, perhaps hundreds of items—bags, packages, hats, umbrellas—hanging from hooks and all systematically arranged. He went right to her camera and, with a very polite bow, passed it across the counter.

PLOT LINES

Asahi is the word for "rising sun." You see it most often nowadays on beer bottles and on the sidewalk vending machines down along Kokutai-doro Street that dispense the cans and the bottles, short and tall. When I was a kid going to war movies in San Francisco and listening to the radio newscasters, a rising sun was the emblem of the enemy. A vivid red globe on a field of white was as loathsome as the swastika, synonymous with deceit, immoral aggression, invasion from afar.

This old symbology is not lost on Michael Crichton, whose new novel recently arrived here in the mail. It's a very good tale, at the plotting level, suspenseful and highly charged, but very troubling too for the way he depicts, or fails to depict, the Japanese.

Rising Sun is designed as a murder mystery, set in L.A., opening on the night a huge corporation called Nakamoto celebrates the completion of its new headquarters building. Festivities are disrupted when the body of a young American woman is found dead on the conference table in a meeting room on one of the upper floors. The central characters are two L.A. cops called in to investigate. Lieutenant Peter Smith was recently appointed as a special liaison for cases involving Japanese in Los Angeles. Captain John Conner is a veteran officer who has lived in Tokyo, bilingual, bicultural.

So far, so good. In American fiction bicultural white guys are still in short supply. Before long we get to know these officers very well, in part because Peter Smith tells the story. Here he is, in chapter 1, introducing himself.

> Actually I was sitting on my bed in my apartment in Culver City, watching the Lakers game with the sound turned off, while I tried to study vocabulary for my introductory Japanese class.
>
> It was a quiet evening, I had gotten my daughter to sleep about eight. Now I had the cassette player on the bed, and the cheerful woman's voice was saying things like "Hello, I am a police officer. Can I be of assistance?" and "Please show me the menu."[3]

What do we learn here? In just a few lines we learn quite a bit. He lives in an apartment, not a house. He is studying a foreign language, not common for an American cop. He follows basketball. He has a daughter who must be young because she goes to bed at eight, and he is the one who *put* her to bed, so this is a father who helps care for his child. Perhaps he is a single father. We don't know for sure, but it feels that way. In short, we have a careful selection of small details that quickly begin to establish Peter Smith as a vulnerable human being with a *life*.

Now consider page 23, where we meet Kasaguro Ishigura, the first Japanese character to be introduced and an important one for the story, a corporate attorney for Nakamoto and, in the novel, the corporation's main spokesman:

> Ishigura took my card with one hand and said, "Is this your home phone, detective?" I was surprised. He spoke the kind of unaccented English you can only learn by living here for a long time, starting when you're young. He must have gone to school here. One of the thousands of Japanese who studied in America in the seventies. When they were sending 150,000 students a year to America, to learn about our country. And we were sending 200 American students a year to Japan.

These figures are accurate. But what do they tell us about Ishigura? They tell me that he is not so much a character in this novel as he is a statistic or a sociological case study. It is an odd kind of information to give us in a work of fiction, especially in the first scene with an ongoing character. But in *Rising Sun* it is typical information. Repeatedly, the presentation of Japanese habits and values comes to us in the form of numbers, generalities, speeches and sermons by Captain Conner, various professors, TV reporters, and engineers whose lives have been affected by Japanese business practice.

Along the way the unraveling of the crime has considerable appeal. It is complex, with some rich detail about recent video technology and the bizarre sexual tastes of the victim. In the end Ishigura is revealed as the killer. He has tried to cover up the crime in order to protect his company and turn the murder to the corporation's advantage. But he never becomes more than a two-dimensional kind of hit man. We never learn the kinds of things we learn about Peter Smith. We never find out where Ishigura went to school, or where he lives, what kind of neighborhood, whether in a house or in a condo, whether or not he has a family—a wife? some kids?—or follows sports, or what he likes to eat, details that could begin to put a reader in closer touch with the realities of a life.

No Japanese character in *Rising Sun* comes close to being as fully depicted or as engaging as Smith and Conner. Throughout the novel there is an intimacy with the American characters that is missing with the Japanese, who are kept at a distance. We get a lot of sociology about them, and economic history, but we do not get what a novel with this kind of ambition ought to provide for us: a fleshed-out Asian character whose life conveys some human depth and complexity.

What *Rising Sun* gives us are several corporate types and page after page about the forces that have made the murder significant, forces referred to variously as *Japan, the Asian Community, the Japanese Mind,* and most often *the Japanese.* Crichton uses this term over and over and over, referring sometimes to officers of Nakamoto Corporation, sometimes to a group of investors who have gained control of the American economy, sometimes to an unspecified power bloc that can influence American media, federal policy, and law enforcement. Sometimes *the Japanese* refers to the character and priorities of an entire population. By the end the term comes to refer to all of these simultaneously; and the adversary then is not a person, it is not Ishigura, nor is it the corporation. It is a faceless and monolithic threat from somewhere across the water.

Such treatment of Asians in American fiction has been going on for quite some time, for a century or more. So is it more troublesome now than it has been in the past? Well, yes, since the world is getting smaller day by day, and the need to understand and recognize one another at the human level grows ever more urgent, and fiction is one of the ways we have invented for exchanging information on what it's like to be a human being, how it feels outside and in. But what we get in *Rising Sun* is yet another version of that emblematic red-and-white flag from World War II. At a time of high-pitched national anxiety about the economic future, a master storyteller uses his skills to humanize the Americans, while the Japanese emerge as a collective, conniving, and still unfathomable opponent.

Reading it here in Fukuoka just quickens the sense of irony and overkill. I look out the window at the looming gray skies above the close-packed rows of buildings that line the hillside above us, where families are squeezed into their diminutive apartments, and I think about the final scene.

The crime is solved. Lieutenant Peter Smith is heading home, a disillusioned professional, his future uncertain, and now he sees his L.A. neighborhood as if for the first time. The tree-lined street that used to look pleasant enough doesn't look so good anymore. Things are actually falling apart. The city is layered with smog. The freeway is uneven and bumpy, with overhead signs spray painted by gangs. "The air was bad and the street seemed dirty," and somehow—since this scene concludes a 343-page indictment—the streets themselves will continue to deteriorate if we don't do something soon about *the Japanese.*

I look out the window and imagine Peter Smith's counterpart, a police lieutenant here on the island of Kyushu, driving home at the end of an exhausting week. He would be faced with a similar prospect. He would not see graffiti sprayed on the overpass, but he would be worrying about his daughter's future, and he would have bumpy streets to contend with, under-maintained, and skies dense with pollution, and avenues of run-down, black-streaked concrete buildings built too fast in the early 1960s when there was a rush, all over Japan, to pump up the infrastructure. His apartment would be smaller than Smith's, and his car too, if he owned one, in this city where you can't purchase a car until you show proof that you have a place to park it.

UNFORGETTABLE

Only 20 percent of Japanese families own more
than one auto compared with 65 percent in the US.
— *Money Magazine,* October 1991

I feel compelled to include this dinner party we were invited to a while back, where I had the chance to talk with a fellow who sounds a lot like one of our neighbors in the States. He watches the concentration of money in the hands of a few very powerful families and consortiums, and he doesn't like the effects of this. Property values go up and up. He works longer hours with fewer rewards awaiting him in the future.

"Nobody in Japan can buy a house now," he says. "My parents have this house. But the younger people . . . everyone works long hours, and we save our money. We are all very good about saving money, as you know. I don't remember the percentages. Better than in the US, I think. But what difference does it make? We are supposed to be one of the richest nations in the world. This is what you hear today. But what is 'rich'? What does it mean to be rich when you can work for your entire life and not be able to earn enough money to buy a house?"

I will call him Reijiro. We are sitting on tatami mats on the floor of his family's dining room, around a low wooden table inlaid with mother-of-pearl. He is a slender fellow, as are most young Japanese men. Except among the wrestlers, you seldom see obesity here, male or female, seldom see anyone you would call "heavy." Reijiro has a narrow waist, wide shoulders, slightly curly hair (perhaps some family gene from Okinawa).

His eyes are full of questions. He doesn't speak much English, but his sister does. She studied it for years, and for a while she dated an American man from Texas. She translates what her brother can't say. The sister, Kimiko, is twenty-eight. Reijiro is thirty. He works in a camera shop. She does clerical work and moonlights nights at a karaoke bar. Neither of them has married yet. Neither owns a car. They use subways and buses. They both still live at home because it's cheaper. The father isn't here much. He spends most of his time in Tokyo. A businessman, they say. Sometimes they don't see him for six or seven months. It was an arranged marriage, so the mother and the father have never been close. "No love," Kimiko will tell us later on.

Information trickles out during an hour or so of sipping sake. They are friends of some friends, and they have invited us for a dinner toward the end of the season the Japanese call "Forget the Year." It corresponds roughly to our Christmas season and occupies most of December. They are intrigued with the idea of getting to know some Americans, who are not as visible here as in Tokyo and Kyoto. Maybe the cultural mixture appeals to them too. Jeanne has brought a conversation pocket dictionary, which she holds in her lap for ready reference. So we are laughing and sipping and groping along in a kind of broken bilingual chatter, which grows easier after the sake cups have been refilled a few times.

No one in the family has been to America, but they have seen the films and a lot of TV coverage and they have listened to the songs. They want to know how many cars we have. They want to know what we think about Japan. They want to know about our families. They tell us about theirs. In the room where we sit, half of one wall is occupied by the family altar. Two folding doors stand open to reveal shelving decorated with gold leaf, a golden Buddha, columns of fresh chrysanthemums. Above a low table with candles and with incense sticks in a bowl, there are small framed photos of grandparents and great-grandparents. On another wall, directly above our heads, hang larger portraits of the grandparents wearing traditional dress, kimono and yukata. Beside these, a framed panel shows their names in thick black calligraphy, and over each name a grandparent has left a red handprint, thread lines of white across the palms. They preside over the afternoon and evening and all the food and drink we are about to consume—the ancestral portraits and the bright red prints of the hands of the grandparents who have been dead for many years.

After an hour of sipping, the food begins to appear, one dish at a time, delivered from the kitchen by the gracious and self-effacing mother, who bows and mutters an apology each time she sets something fabulous before us. It is odd to watch this. Kimiko the daughter is outspoken, bold, vivacious. She usually wears jeans, leather jacket, scarlet lipstick. Today it's a smart blouse and miniskirt. She pours our sake with a geisha bow that is also a parody of a geisha bow, having some fun with the tradition of the subservient female.

"Jim-san, Jeanne-san," says Kimiko with a playful smirk and a glance at our empty cups, "we are honored that our Fukuoka sake pleases you so much."

She is in a way imitating her mother, yet not mocking her. They both enjoy the daughter's little game. The mother dresses in a plainer, older style of western clothing, slacks, a simple sweater. Not dowdy, but more sedate. There are probably kimonos hanging in a closet somewhere, but this is not a kimono day. You seldom see them now, unless it's a formal occasion, like the photos the grandparents posed for, or New Year's at the local shrine, when everyone in the neighborhood is out buying good-luck charms, burning last year's charms, and promenading in the courtyard. Later we learn that the mother, Nobu-san, grew up on a farm in this region, where her people have lived and farmed for a thousand years. Her parents negotiated with a well-to-do city family, so she had married "up," as they say, the first from her family to leave the countryside and move into town.

We start with *tsukemono*, homemade by Nobu-san, bits of pickled carrot, turnip, cucumber. Then comes roe of halibut, clusters of golden fish eggs. We have salty/sweet black beans the size of peanuts and cooked to be eaten like peanuts, one at a time. We have strips of salmon, an inch or so wide and rolled into bite-size morsels, and daikon that has been cooked in a broth of beef and beef gristle, and tiny shrimp, their bodies the size of the end of your finger, fried spicy and eaten whole, and beef seared on the outside, still raw at the center, and another kind of fish egg, very small and red, smaller than pinheads and presented with thin-sliced squid. And there are glistening silver shrimp about eight inches long, served alive, so that their feelers are still waving around as the platter is set upon the table. On their undersides the tentacles are flailing. The idea is to select one, break off the head, peel the skin immediately, and eat the raw, living flesh.

Jeanne and I are not squeamish about exotic dishes, but we can't go this far. I identify with the shrimp, squirming as if they know their minutes are numbered. But Nobu-san, the self-effacing mother who has prepared most of this food back in the kitchen with the help of her microwave, has now joined us at the table. She has emptied her first cup of sake, poured by Kimiko. She gestures for another, then reaches with both hands and breaks off a shrimp's head, dips the flesh into her side dish of soy sauce and horse-radish, and announces in her soft, motherly voice that this is indeed *"Oishi."* Delicious.

It is about this time that a second platoon of visitors shows up, friends of the family, a man named Kato, with his wife and their fifteen-year-old son. Kato looks about forty-five, a muscular fellow with a rascal glint in his eye. He is a marble cutter who was once a fisherman. He has brought along some sashimi, a specialty from the small offshore island where he grew up. His wife carries a platter of what smells like Kentucky Fried Chicken.

Kato's older son is a sumo wrestler who did well in the recent tournament. This is like having a son playing in the NFL. He is the proudest of fathers, was probably something of an athlete himself in his day. We pass around some photos of the husky, bulging son, while Kato and his wife begin to catch up with the party by downing two fast shots each from a quart of Johnny Walker red label that has appeared from somewhere. He wants to know if I speak any Japanese.

"*Sumi-ma-sen,*" I say. "*Nihongo-ga wakari-ma-sen.*" ("Please forgive me, I don't know any Japanese.")

He gazes across the table for a moment, as if deciding how to handle this. At last he says, "*Como está?*"

"*Muy bien,*" I say.

"*Habla Español?*"

"*Un poco,*" I say.

"*Si, muy poco,*" he says with a laugh, pointing a finger at himself, at the tip of his nose.

He bites off some sashimi and takes a long pull of the Johnny Walker and says, "*Parlez-vous Français?*"

"*Un petit peu,*" I say.

"*Voulez vous de cognac?*" he says, lifting the bottle.

"*Merci, non,*" I say, pointing to the sake.

"Ah. Sake," says Kato, framing his face with widespread fingers.

I look at Kimiko to translate.

"Makes your eyes bright," she says.

As a young man Kato lived for four years in the Canary Islands, he explains, via Kimiko, so he has met fishermen from all around the Mediterranean. "*Molto bono,*" he says, pointing to his platter of Kentucky Fried.

While the chicken and the sashimi are making the rounds, one of the long silver shrimp leaps into the air, startling everyone. It has been lying there for half an hour as if dead. Suddenly it springs to life, makes a twitching arc across the table, and lands on another platter a foot and a half away. Kato-san takes it as a sign that this shrimp's moment has finally come. He grabs it and breaks the head off and peels the shell from the body. He dips the quivering flesh into his little cup of sauce and gives it a gleeful chomp.

"*Oishi-des,*" says the mother. ("It's tasty, eh.")

"*Muchas gracias,*" says Kato with his rascal smile. Many graces. Much thanks. To the shrimp. To the whiskey. To the hostess-cook.

Reijiro decides it is music time. He rises from the table, slides back a shoji screen decorated with a garden scene, bonsai trees, a rippling brook. In the next room he has what looks like a thousand-dollar sound system. He wants to know if we recognize the voice on his newest CD. He comes back in and stands watching us, awaiting our reactions, as we listen.

It's a new reissue of Bobby Vinton singing "Blue Velvet." When I tell him Jeanne and I grew up with Bobby and that there will always be a place in our hearts for this song, a huge grin fills his face.

Again he slips past the shoji screen. "Blue Velvet" fades away. The next thing we hear is Natalie Cole singing "The Very Thought of You." I tell Reijiro we grew up with this song too, but we love it even more.

"Arigato go-zai-mas," I say with a low bow to the table. ("Thank you very much.")

At this he bows deeply from the waist, grateful that I have allowed him to please us with this choice of song. Kimiko tells us it is his CD of the season, his "most favorite."

"Domo," he says. *"Domo arigato go-zai-mashi*ta!" ("My gratitude runneth over.")

This is of course the hit collection *Unforgettable,* featuring all of Nat King Cole's great tunes from the 1940s and '50s as re-sung by his daughter. What astounds us is that everyone at the table knows the words to all these songs— Kato the marble cutter who once lived in the Canary Islands, and Kato's wife and their fifteen-year-old son who, until this song, has not opened his mouth, and Kimiko, age twenty-eight, the daughter who once dated a man from Texas, and Reijiro, age thirty, who claims to know very little English, and Nobu-san, the fifty-five-year-old mother who knows no English at all. When "Mona Lisa" comes on, Nobu's lips begin to move, as she sings quietly to herself. Pretty soon everyone's lips are moving, humming.

I don't think what happens next could have happened much earlier. Without a few drinks to loosen everyone up, they would not be willing to sing aloud in front of their American visitors and risk humiliation for mispronouncing words. But now some time has passed. Some trust has accumulated. To the kinship that comes with food and drink, we are ready to add the kinship of song. One by one we start singing along with the recording, led by Kato-san and by Reijiro, who can hardly contain his passion for these lyrics.

"Mona Risa, Mona Risa, men have name you. You so rike a raydee wis a mystic smire . . ."

By the time the album's title song comes through the speakers, some kind of dreamy-eyed, head-wagging nostalgia has taken over the room. They mouth these tunes and hum along with an amazing mix of familiarity and affection. We are all swaying with the melody of "Unforgettable," as if the double-track voices of the famous father and the devoted daughter singing this early '50s classic has transported them all back to the same high school dances Jeanne and I carry around in our personal data banks of pop song memories. Not to that exact place in the memory bank. But maybe somewhere similar.

That's how it looks and feels, at any rate. You never know for sure what's running through another person's mind. You can only guess. Are they just acting dreamy-eyed to make us feel at home? According to the legend, the Japanese are supposed to be inscrutable, mysterious, and governed by rules we westerners will never understand, the kind of people who will sooner or later sneak up on you when you least expect it. But I have a hunch that just the opposite may be true, given the way the world is going.

Maybe they are starting to remind us of someone we know too well. They love to eat. They love to sing and party. They love to drink. They drink more than is good for them. They get sentimental. They are shameless consumers. They wear jeans and running shoes and ball caps. They line up at McDonald's. They are sports nuts and media nuts. They love high-tech equipment. They covet brand names. Meanwhile, their political leaders move in and out of the corporate power structure, in and out of favor, in and out of scandal and disgrace. Maybe the Japanese are a little too familiar now, like a brother you grew up with who learned whatever he knows from the same place you learned it, and when he annoys you it is because he reminds you of yourself.

When the song ends, and our voices subside, Kato-san bows with a silly grin and says, *"Muchas gracias. Très bien."*

We all break into loud applause. For Nat. For Natalie. For Reijiro's CD. For the black beans and the sashimi and the Kentucky Fried Chicken and the strips of salmon and the salty, savory fingertip shrimp, for the Fukuoka sake and the Johnny Walker and the spectacle of the long silver cylinders of shrimp still wiggling on their platter. We applaud the mother who has prepared this feast, whose family has farmed the same farm for a thousand years, and the grandparents too, who have watched and listened from the gold-leafed altar and from the wall overhead, their bold red handprints shining as if the ink were wet and fresh.

THE MIDNIGHT
NOODLE POT

Three more days and I'll be gone, leaving Jeanne to her fellowship, while I do some island-hopping. Right now we're waiting for the rain to break, so we can plunge into the three-sweater, two-jacket wind blowing in from the Tsushima Straits. There's a long list of things to check off before I catch the plane, starting with a hike to the city art museum, over by Ohori Park, for one more look at the traveling show of original prints by the *ukiyo-e* masters Hiroshige, Hokusai, et al.

No matter how cold it is, the joggers will be out there circling the park in teams—headbands, shorts, and T-shirts—in defiance of all known human thresholds of pain. But the rain and the wind together is a lot to put up with, if you don't absolutely have to be outside. It keeps us close to the heater, and I'm thinking I have to finish the story of what happened later that night, after dinner. If somebody had been leaving the next day, this would have made a pretty good farewell party.

The Natalie Cole CD had only whetted our appetite for song. Kato-san wanted more. We all wanted more. He insisted that we travel across town with him to a karaoke club where he happens to be a member. Before long we were trooping through the house, past walls of shoji screens, down the hardwood corridors, pausing to step back into our shoes lined up in the entryway, then out into the chilly night, four in Kato's car, four in a cab.

This was not a club where you sit in a row of padded chairs with other men while the mama-sans behind the bar serve drinks and make attentive conversation. I have been to one of those, where an American friend has his own bottle of Courvoisier waiting on a shelf with his name written on a little tag that hangs around the neck. At Mr. Kato's club, called Sharps and Flats, you reserve a private room, which he had done before we left the house.

An elevator took us to the third floor. More drinks were ordered, more food, snacks for munching, mini-sandwiches, sushi, crackers, bits of fish, while we began to scan the many pages of song titles deciding what to sing and who should go first. The catalogue was a spiral binder, with dozens of pages encased in plastic, and on each page dozens of titles. There must have been a thousand, including several columns of American titles, but most were Japanese.

Along the wall little prisms caught spotlight beams and turned them into streaks of purple, blue, and yellow. Overhead a glass ball twirled, as if this were an old-time dance hall. The ceiling and the walls were alive with swirling, sparkling lights. Cushioned seats lined two sides of the room, so everyone had a view of the big video monitor in the corner where the ideograms would soon be floating past, below the three-minute dramas acting out the stories of the songs.

In the corner opposite the monitor there was a small stage, with two mike stands, two very good detachable mikes, and a smaller monitor for the singer to watch. Between the big screen and the stage there was a large, black, dial-clustered song selection console, with one dial for pitch control, so that if you come in above or below the background orchestra, you only lose a note or two before the track is adjusted to your voice. Basic to the idea of karaoke is that everyone should get that three minutes in the spotlight we all deserve, and that everyone should sound good, or at least better than you thought you could sound.

Nobu-san is persuaded to go first, as a way of showing respect for age and motherhood and family. From the loose-leaf binder she chooses a song.

Kimiko works the remote switch, punches in the number that triggers the console. About the time Nobu steps onto the stage, the video kicks in, with a little overture to a mournful ballad about departure and grief. A line of ideograms moves across the bottom of the screen. We watch images of women weeping at the dock while a troopship pulls away. There are melancholy pans of open water, birds in lonesome flight, solitary women walking, thinking, waiting, gazing across empty meadows.

One great advantage of video-supported karaoke is that you don't have to understand Japanese to follow the song. The pictures are here to guide you. In this case, the mournful edge on Nobu's voice is here to guide you too. Is she perhaps thinking of someone lost in the war? A father? A brother? Or is she thinking of the absent husband who never comes home from Tokyo? Or of some other man she might have married if her life had gone another way? Beneath the nasal whine and throat-constricting warble, the grief in her voice is powerful and raw.

I find myself thinking of Emmy Lou Harris and Tammy Wynette. I think of Hank Williams singing "I'm So Lonesome I Could Cry." A lot of these Japanese popular songs are like country western ballads, tales of yearning, remorse, betrayal, the gains and losses of the heart. The best singers are the ones who make you believe that they believe in the sentiment, no matter how sentimental. In one of Conway Twitty's songs there is a line that goes, "You got to sing like you don't need the money / You got to love like you'll never get hurt." That's how Nobu-san sings it for us, with just the right blend of vibrato and held-in passion, and still wearing her overcoat buttoned, as if she plans to sing this one tune and walk back out the door.

When her song ends we all applaud wildly. Then Kato-san takes the stage. He is equally emotional but in a stalwart and stoic way. His song is very manly, and one he knows well, a song he has no doubt sung here and elsewhere hundreds of times. His chest swells. He becomes a warrior, gazing past the monitor, singing with the voice of a man who has walked through fire, while on the screen we watch samurai swordsmen with their hair in topknots.

A young man challenges an older man, whose face fills with dread. The older man, a noble who has for some reason lost his pride and his stature, needs to be protected by his vassals. They are also terrified, but surround him out of duty. Everyone but the young man is frantic. The older man flees. Gruff swordsmen come and go, running, grasping their hilts. Finally there is a fight, and the agony of hara-kiri, as a warrior plunges a knife into his own belly. There is disgrace mixed with dignity, with sacrifice, tragedy, and valor, all revealed in the tragic and valorous samurai face of Kato-san, whose throat swells, pressing at his collar, as the song's last piercing note fills the room. His head drops in a warrior's bow.

Now Kimiko takes the stage in her high heels, her high-waisted leather jacket. She has chosen a very upbeat contemporary tune about young love in the big city. The band is jazzier, the drumming insistent. Kimiko belts it as if this is the audition for a musical and she has one shot at the big time.

On-screen we see Tokyo from overhead, from a helicopter swinging around the high-rises. A svelte young woman in miniskirt is striding along the boulevard. Close up on her face, the contained and solitary grace, not revealing much to those she walks among, but we know she is looking for something, she is poised and ready, looking for Mister Right, perhaps for the man from Texas who was here for a year, then flew away, transferred to Singapore.

Her brother Reijiro chooses a dreamy song of erotic longing. He is a sly and slender fellow. As a singer he is soft-voiced, rather modest, not looking at the rest of us. On the mini-stage he is a reluctant celebrity keeping his eyes on the big screen where a female body begins to writhe and squirm, rolling out from under a sheet so that her legs are revealed, then her bare bottom. Cut to the neck where her hands begin a long massage downward, pushing the sheet away from her breasts. She is alone, in the midst of some kind of fantasy or waking dream, remembering the past, remembering a day when she is out at the cliff edge, walking above the beach, in the wind. Cut back and forth. From the cliff. To the bed. To the cliff. But mostly the bed.

Everyone is amused by this choice, including Nobu-san, Reijiro's mother. Kato turns to me, laughing, and says, with his rascal grin, *"Sumi-ma-sen. Pardonnez-moi."* ("Please forgive us for exposing you and your wife to such a spectacle.")

He holds a hand over his eyes, with two fingers parted, so he can peek through and continue watching.

Reijiro's face is solemn. What is he thinking of? Perhaps nothing. He has been sipping sake steadily for the past four hours. Does he have a girlfriend? We didn't ask. Camera bug. CD collector. Like this screen-girl, is he too a lonely fantasizer? What's going through his mind as he stands here singing deadpan lyrics to these fleshy scenes?

He gets a big hand, stepping off the stage, heading back to his glass, and I know my turn has come. I have been flipping through the catalog, scanning the American list. In this members-only club, where foreigners are seldom seen, there are eighty or a hundred to choose from. Jazz standards. Old favorites. Hawaiian and country tunes. "Beyond the Reef." "Paper Moon." "Heartbreak Hotel." I finally find one I think I can deliver with the right amount of commitment, and tell Kimiko to punch in "The Tennessee Waltz."

Moments later it is coming through the speakers, with a sound track off the Patti Page arrangement from the early '50s. On the screen we see a dance hall somewhere in Nashville or Oak Ridge. A tall fellow dressed in jeans and boots and rodeo shirt is doing the two-step with a good looking young woman, while another fellow is moving through the crowd to cut in. The second fellow twirls away with the woman . . . and the rest is history. For the trio on the dance floor—and also for me, since my grandmother happened to come from the mountains of eastern Tennessee. You might say I learned to sing from her when she was still living with us in San Francisco, puttering around the house, humming her old mountain favorites, like "The Crawdad Song" and "Three Black Crows." My grandmother didn't know "The Tennessee Waltz." That came after her time for learning songs. But her voice is still alive in my nervous system, along with all the nights we listened to the Grand Ol' Opry booming through the house during my growing-up years. So I know how to do this particular song with a mountain edge and the proper sentiment for the melancholy fellow telling the tale.

To the surprise of everyone here but me, Jeanne can also sing this song with fervor, because she too grew up with Hank Williams and Lefty Frizzell and Patti Page and Bob Wills and the Texas Playboys. After the war, after the camps closed, she and her family were transplanted to a housing project called Cabrillo Homes, where people from many backgrounds found themselves trying to survive, among them numerous families from the South and Southwest who had come to the coast to work in the shipyards and aircraft plants—families much like mine, except that this was Long Beach, instead of San Francisco. In those days her father was still playing the banjo-like *samisen* and the *shakuhachi* flute. But Jeanne, at age eleven, was humming other tunes, listening to country voices blaring out of the windows of apartments upstairs and across the block.

So here we are, on the third floor of the Sharps and Flats Club in midtown Fukuoka toward the end of the season they call "Forget the Year," singing "The Tennessee Waltz," then "Jambalaya," then "Don't Fence Me In."

Before the applause subsides, Kato is calling out, "Jim-san, Jeanne-san! The Saints. The Saints!"

I look at Kimiko for guidance, and she is nodding in agreement. "Yes, yes! The Saints Go Marching In!"

I haven't seen it in the catalog, I tell her, holding up my copy of the English-language pages.

"Oh," she says, "it's not there. It's on the Japanese list, but the words all in English anyway." It is a perennial karaoke favorite, she tells me. "We love this song so much!"

"Why this one?" I ask.

"*So* American," she says.

They are all smiling now, urging us with their smiles to agree to sing one more.

"We will help you," says Nobu-san.

"*Merci beaucoup*," says Kato in advance.

"The Saints!" they cry. "The Saints! The Saints!"

The video comes on. A Dixieland band somewhere in New Orleans belts out two tight choruses, big fat tuba, with a cornet punching at the melody. As lyrics begin to flow across the screen, Jeanne and I take the lead, while the others call out echo lines.

"When the Saints . . ."

"Oh when the Saints!"

"Go marching in . . ."

"Go marching in!"

It is scored as a parade song. The on-screen band struts along a street lined with happy spectators. In our private room they are all on their feet now, dancing and waving their arms, belting out the lyrics—Kimiko, Reijiro, Nobu-san, and Kato and Kato's wife and the fifteen-year-old son. They cheer when the music swells and the band from Bourbon Street is back for another chorus, trombone, clarinet, the raucous banjo *chunk chunk chunk*.

"How I long to be in that number," we cry, "when the Saints go marching in . . ."

"MARCHING IN!"

The band fades out, cornets and trombones heading back to Dixie. Applause and laughter fills the room, then the voices subside as we fall into our seats, wondering what can happen now.

With a silly grin Kato-san bows toward us. *"Arigato. Molto bono. Très bien."*

He is not sitting down. He knows this is as much as we can hope to get from Sharps and Flats. He is already into his sport coat, knocking back the last of his drink, urging his wife and son and the rest of us toward the door, a samurai general moving his troops. Into the corridor. Down the elevators. Call a cab. Follow me, he says, and we are driving again, back the way we came, at high speed, since the hour is late and the streets are clear. His destination is a noodle shop, its front door covered by hanging banners. We duck under the banners and into a room filled with steam and twenty sweating people squeezed in around low tables.

One empty table seems to have enough space for three or four of us, but somehow we all gang around it, on the floor, shoulder to shoulder. Ramen is the specialty here, served in large steaming bowls. You use chopsticks and bend over the bowl. The noodles are long and slick and must be inhaled, so making a lot of noise is okay. In fact, if you are a visitor and don't make some noise they worry that you aren't having a good time, especially at this time of night, when the guards are down.

Kato points to his bowl, then to his stomach, then to his head, rolling his eyes like a cartoon drunk. "Tomorrow. Okay."

"Eat the noodles tonight?" I say. "No headache in the morning?"

"Si, como no."

"You like?" says Kimiko.

"Oishi-des" ("delicious"), says Jeanne, who is in heaven in a place like this, transported back once again to the childhood days of family crowd scenes in Inglewood and Santa Monica.

I have my heated face down close to the bowl in front of me—we are all glistening, slurping up the ramen—and I'm thinking about steam and about the songs we have sung, how both songs and steam can open so many different kinds of portals. It rises off the bowls on all the tables and from the hidden pools at Yufuin, and from the dark sand at Ibusuki, and from the top of Sakurajima, and from the wrinkled floor of Kilauea on the midocean island of Hawai'i, and from the hot springs all up and down the Coast Range and the Cascades, and from the stove over there across the room where the cook in his white apron perspires and the stainless steel noodle pot is simmering. They too must have a place in what is called the Ring of Fire. The cook. The brimming midnight noodle pot. The steaming world.

BLACK ROCKS,
ANCIENT VOICES

HONOLULU,
VOLCANO,
KONA,
KOHALA

He ali'i ka 'aina; he kauwa ke kanaka.
(The land is a chief; man is its servant.)
— Mary Kawena Pukui, *'Olelo No'eau* (1983)

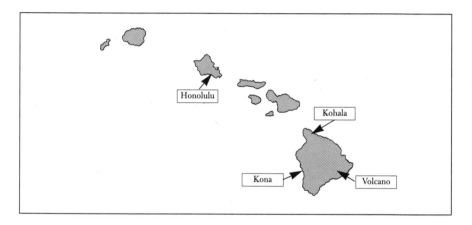

Hawaii. Surrounded by the Pacific Ocean. Alaska's Aleutian Islands are far to the north, Samoa and Polynesia far to the south. Mexcio is due east, Taiwan due west.

MELODY LINES

My father grew up in a Texas farm town, working cotton every summer in the dry, relentless heat. To escape, he joined the navy, and they sent him west, first to San Diego, then farther west, on out to Pearl Harbor with a submarine crew. This was in the 1920s. On my wall here in Santa Cruz I have a picture that shows him in his navy whites, holding in his lap a Hawaiian steel guitar, young guy from Texas, somewhere in Honolulu two decades before the bombs fell and the ship-filled harbor turned to flame.

I don't know for sure what happened to him over there. He never talked about it much, partly because he never talked about anything much. But something gave those years a shine. My guess is they were magic years. The islands have quite a bit of magic even now. Imagine what it was like seventy years ago, before statehood, before tourism, before the megahotels went up. He was eighteen, nineteen, twenty. He learned to play the steel guitar when it was still a new instrument, invented by Hawaiians and introduced to the world not long before he got there. He fell in love with the picks and the strings and the sliding steel bar and the sweet music they could make. He learned a small repertoire of island tunes that filled our house when I was a kid growing up in San Francisco.

He spent a couple of years out there, then he went back home. But after the places he'd seen, the land east of Dallas looked pretty bleached and dry. Steady pay was harder and harder to find. By the time he met my mother, he was work-

ing as a field hand in the Texas panhandle, at the outer edges of what was called "the Dust Bowl," cropland country where the soil was wearing thin. When he left Texas this time, he was gone for good.

On one of his navy cruises he'd seen the city by the Golden Gate, and that's where they headed. Before long he'd found work painting houses. Four or five years went by, and he'd saved enough to put some money down on a little place in the Sunset District, not far from Ocean Beach. Half a block from our house you could stand on the corner and sight due west down the long slope of Irving Street, and see a wedge of the Pacific he once had crossed and dreamed of crossing again, sometime, somehow.

❦

In one of my earliest memories from our years in that neighborhood my father is down on his knees in front of the radio. We had one of those old-time radios made of dark carved wood, with a curving top and cloth over the speaker, a piece of furniture large enough to dominate the room. Set against a wall by itself, it looked like an altar. In those pre-TV days, if you had seen our family gathered around it staring at the speaker as we listened to an evening program like "Suspense," you might have thought it was an altar to the Deities of Sound.

Kneeling there alone on a Saturday afternoon my father would hold his ear up close to the cloth and fool with the dials, trying to bring in a program known as "Hawai'i Calls" that used to be broadcast live from the lanai of the Moana Hotel. With a mike down close to the surf, the M.C. would remind you seductively that "The temperature of the air here at Waikiki is seventy-six, the temperature of the water is seventy-four." Sometimes Lena Machado, known as "Hawai'i's Song Bird," would sing; sometimes the great falsetto artist George Kainapau. Some Saturdays the signal would be so faint it was nothing more than a thin and lonesome trickle. Every once in a while, if the weather was right, you could hear the songs and the voices loud and clear, the ukes, the rhythm guitars, and somewhere behind the music the lapping surf.

He would wait all week for this. He would sit back on his heels and listen reverently. Afterward he would plug in his amp and hook up his steel and spend an hour or two working on "Green Rose Hula" or "The Hilo March," upbeat, full of slides and chimes. The picks would flash and the strings would whine, and you could not interrupt him then. Even a call to dinner could not break his concentration. Nothing could come between him and his strings. I often tried, as a kid will do, wondering what his daddy is up to. And I would take his scowl of irritation personally. I know better now.

This was toward the end of the Depression. He was working ten- and twelve-hour days just to stay even. By that time he had his painting contractor's license and a three-man crew. He had a payroll to meet and a truck to run and a mortgage and two kids to feed. I know now that the tunes he played and the old radio show he waited for kept him connected to a time and a place in his life he always dreamed of getting back to and never could.

It took me quite a while to realize that my own interest in what lay farther west was kindled right there, in our living room in the Sunset District of San Francisco. Anything that brings your father to his knees is going to make an impression on you. And that was what could do it, the sound, or the very hope of hearing the sound of island music, trickling across the water from twenty-four hundred miles away.

🌿

I flew to Hawai'i the first time right after college, thinking then that this was an original idea for an expedition. I was so busy setting out on my own, I had not stopped to remember the sound of his guitar and where he'd learned to play it. But I have heard it more and more in the years since he passed away. I hear it now, "The Hilo March," as I study this old photograph of the young fellow from east Texas in his navy whites, and I wonder if he himself ever got to Hilo. He could have, though he never mentioned it. There's no way to know for sure. Maybe this song was just in the air. Most Hawaiian songs pay tribute to a specific place, a town, a bay, a mountain, a point of land. Maybe he had heard the '20s recording that first made it famous, a steel guitar version by Pale K. Lua, and it worked on him the way it has worked on me.

The first trip took fourteen hours, on a propeller-powered flight from San Francisco. En route I was dreaming of beaches, but I soon found myself drawn inland, toward the mountains and the chain of craters that bear witness to

Hawai'i's origins. Like a chain of stop-time photographs, they chart the history of the earth, from Kaua'i in the north, to Hawai'i in the south, the Big Island, the youngest and still growing. That is the island I prefer to visit now. Hilo happens to be the principal town, a port town on the windward side. The Big Island has produced many talented musicians and composers. The best slack-key guitar players have come from there. I like to go into the high country and sit a while among the plains and heaps of old dark lava and listen to the stillness of the craters, then come down into town and listen to the music, always listening for some note I must have heard once, or more than once, or maybe something in between the notes he was picking on the silvery strings that held him captivated after he had switched off the radio and sat down to practice on those long-ago Saturday afternoons.

AN ISLAND
DIALOGUE

On my way to the Big Island I stop off in Honolulu to have breakfast with a woman who talks to rocks. She is an eighty-year-old Hawaiian woman with thick white hair and a healer's eyes. Over papaya and coffee she describes a conversation with a very large and influential rock near the town of Nanakuli, on the leeward side of O'ahu, where the county was clearing land for a new dump site.

An odd sequence of events had begun to trouble the construction crew. Tools had unaccountably disappeared. Vehicles were breaking down. A shallow-rooted *keawe* tree had flipped over, doing a kind of somersault. A worker was thrown when a flat stone suddenly upended itself. In Hawai'i, when things like this start to happen, you don't take chances. You seek expert advice, usually from an elder who is in tune with the visible and invisible life of the region. So this woman was called in to look around and see what she could see and feel what she could feel.

"I stood there a while and prayed," she tells me. "And when I opened my eyes I noticed this rock I had not seen at first. It was a large rock, as large as this table"—spreading her hands wide. "I said to that rock, Who are you? And the rock replied that it held the *'aumakua* of that place, the guardian spirit. So I told the workmen that such a rock should not be lying on its side. It should be standing upright, and they did that, they set it up straight. And I went away, thinking that the problem at the dump site had been solved . . ."

This woman's voice, as soft and smooth as a flower petal, has a soothing, mesmerizing quality. As she pauses halfway through her story to signal for more coffee, I am hearing another voice, that of a fellow in my neighborhood at home, who asks me a question each time I get ready to leave for these islands. With a few variations it is always the same question.

"What do you really *do* over there?" he wants to know, his voice tinged with suspicious curiosity.

I never know quite how to reply. He imagines me stretched out on the sand at water's edge sipping mai-tais and baking in the sun for days on end. Thirty-five years ago that image would not have been too far from the truth. On my first trip to these islands the beaches and the surf were powerful magnets. Jeanne and I were married on the beach, with Diamond Head in the distance, and Hawaiian chanting in the air. In those days her black hair hung nearly to her waist. She wore a full-length *muʻumuʻu*. I wore a borrowed aloha shirt. At the surfside ceremony everyone was barefoot. A melting sun had set the sky on fire . . .

So there are sentimental reasons. Nowadays there are also professional reasons. The last time I was accosted by this neighbor of mine, I told him, "If you really want to know, it's a business trip. I have a magazine assignment."

I knew he didn't believe me. That is, he did not believe this was the real reason for the trip. And of course he was right. But I did not know how to tell him this without mentioning the rocks, which would have meant watching his eyes narrow with much more than suspicion. I would have had to watch his face say silently that I was losing my grip. In his world, which is the one most of us inhabit on the mainland—a world ruled by software and satellites and credit cards—rocks do not have powers. They certainly cannot talk. How then could I explain to him that I actually enjoy being in a place where rocks still have a life of their own?

How could I tell him that if I had to name the many things calling me back year after year—the romance, the light, the color, the music, the dance—if I named them all, rocks would be right at the top of the list?

❦

Out near Nanakuli, strange things kept happening. Before long the foreman at the construction site summoned her again. She knew she had to confront that 'aumakua rock, so she went right to it and said, "What do you want?"

"I want to be up higher," the rock replied.

"Why do you want to be up higher?"

"I should not be here. This place is defiled."

The rock, she told them, would have to be moved. The next morning the foreman arrived at her house at 4 AM. "We had to get there and do all the moving before sunup," she explains, "while the energy of the day was on the rise."

When they reached the site, a truck was there, and around it stood ten men from the crew who had also set their alarms for 4 AM. They were waiting to be told where to relocate that rock.

"Up higher," she said, pointing to a ridge. "Up there."

They hoisted it onto the truck bed, and clambered aboard. The truck began to climb, following a little-used road that leads to one of Hawaiian Electric Company's relay stations. They reached the ridge in time to unload the rock before the sun cleared the mountain range behind them. They placed it in a setting of smaller stones, facing west, with a view of the valley below and Oʻahu's leeward shoreline. After the woman blessed the new site and left an offering of ti leaves at the base of the rock, they all drove down the relay station access road, and that was the end of the crew's trouble, as well as the end of her story.

"After that, they didn't have to call me back."

〜

On the mainland this will sound farfetched. But in the volcanically formed and lava-conscious islands of Hawaiʻi you hear such stories all the time. This one happened to be reported on page one of the *Honolulu Advertiser,* which is a very respectable daily, the morning paper for one of the larger cities in the United States. The story was not treated as folklore or as offbeat cult behavior. It was a news feature, with a photo of the relocated rock.

Why was it on page one? Because Hawaiʻi is a place where quite a few people believe it's possible to communicate with rocks. You also find people who claim to communicate with trees, with the wind, and with the mountains, as well as with the creatures who inhabit the mountains and swim in the sea. There is a long tradition for doing this, and in my view these are examples of a very important kind of dialogue—the respectful dialogue between human beings and all the other features of our natural surroundings.

In the world most of us inhabit now, it is easy to lose touch with this dialogue. But when there are stories to remind you that the rock has life, it can help you to remember that the mountain has a life, and the island too. If you are among those who believe the earth itself is a living, breathing organism, whose habits must be recognized and honored, Hawai'i is an excellent place to visit from time to time. While it is now listed among the fifty United States, it continues to be part of Polynesia, connected by a much older set of loyalties to the island clusters farther south—the Marquesas, Samoa, Tonga, Tahiti, the Maori of Aotearoa (sometimes called New Zealand). Polynesians have known all along that these places are alive and need to be listened to.

START AT
THE CENTER

I have seen the craters before, several times, always while passing through, on my way from one side of the island to the other. This time the volcano country is my destination. A couple of miles downslope from the eastern rim of Kilauea, in a rain forest at the untropical altitude of four thousand feet, I have rented a cottage so I can spend my days getting acquainted with the terrain between Hilo and Ka'u, along the island's southern shore.

This is the largest and most southerly island in the chain. According to the Hawaiians, this is where Pele the volcano goddess lives, making her home in the fire pit called Hale-ma'uma'u. Geologists say there is a reservoir of magma stored not far below this fire pit, from which the molten rock pushes outward through tubes and tunnels, looking for somewhere to release the orange curtains and seething rivers. Somewhere down below the reservoir, they say there is a "hot spot," a leak in the huge slab of earth crust known as the Pacific Plate. According to the theory of continental drift, all these islands were formed as the plate drifts inexorably north and west. Successive layers of lava become an underwater seamount that finally pokes through the surface of the sea and then remains volcanic until the creep cuts off access to the hot spot and the magma seeks the next outlet, to build again.

Hawaiians described it another way. They called Hale-ma'uma'u "the navel of the world," a birthplace, the point through which the earth reveals itself.

Many cultures have such navels. The Korean spiritual birthplace is called Chanbaishan, an extinct volcano with a crater lake, near the Chinese border, in the Tumen River region. The Balinese call Mount Agung the navel of the world. For the Wintu in northern California, it is Mount Shasta, the spectacular volcanic peak that still has a hot spring percolating at fourteen thousand feet.

But somehow here—perhaps because the Hawaiian Islands are the most isolated on the planet, the farthest removed from another landmass, where these rocky humps have risen up so close to the center of the wide Pacific—the image has a particular resonance.

Navel.

Axis of the great mandala.

Fiery hub.

A MESSAGE
FROM THE
HOT SPOT

When Mark Twain stopped here in 1866 he wrote back to the *Sacramento Union* that he had seen ". . . bursting, gorgeous sprays of lava-gouts and gem spangles, white, some red, some golden . . . a ceaseless bombardment of unapproachable splendor."

Those fires subsided in 1924, after steam pressure blew out a plug of solidified rock, filled the air with debris and noxious gasses, and more than doubled the crater's size. Pele's fire pit is now about half a mile wide, much quieter than it used to be, approachable now, a scorched and silent place, a sacred place, where the lava is still never very far away. A nostril-stinging sulfur smell surrounds you, leaking from the cracks and fissures along with the thousand plumes of steam. When you're close to a vent, the steam is translucent vapor. Seen from a distance and backlit by the sun, the vapor turns white, sending luminous banners against the gray-black walls.

Think of it as a ring within a ring, in the middle of the Ring of Fire. Halema'uma'u is surrounded by the walls of a larger crater, Kilauea Caldera, a rippled and broken plain shaped like a frying pan. One raw precipice rises in front of you, and beyond that the perfect slope of Mauna Loa—Long Mountain—looms against a cloudless sky.

When locals say this stark and lunar place is Pele's home, they do not speak figuratively. They mean she lives here. I have yet to meet anyone who has been on this island for long, Hawaiian or otherwise, who openly disagrees. I have heard some very levelheaded people claim to have seen her face in the smoke as it billows up from fire fountains to hover above the rift zone. Others tell me they have seen her take human form.

"If you see an old woman hitchhiking," a woman told me the other day, "stop and pick her up and take her wherever she wants to go."

This woman holds a Ph.D. in linguistics from a midwestern campus and has come back home to Hilo to teach at the University of Hawai'i campus here. Thinking she might be kidding, I said, "What if I don't have time to stop?"

She shook her head with a careful smile. "If you don't pick her up, bad luck could come to you. This is the way Madame Pele disguises herself and tests people."

"So you would stop no matter what."

"Let's say it's better to be safe than sorry."

The lip of the fire pit still serves as a kind of altar. Along the ragged edge of heat-scarred rock you will always find recent offerings, left there to honor her and honor the spirit of the place—leis, cut flowers, plates of fruit, the long leaves of the ceremonial ti plant, or a lava rock wrapped in ti leaves.

When I see them I am grateful. I'm glad there is a way to acknowledge whatever resides out here. Whatever it is takes hold of you. The wind. The rock. The expectation. Knowing what churns and boils underground.

Next to a vent I hunker and hold my hands close and feel deep heat hissing up from the restless, bloodred cauldron that once fueled Diamond Head and Maui's Haleakala and Mount Wai'ale'ale on faraway Kaua'i. Call it vapor. Call it a message from the hot spot. Call it the breath of the goddess who dwells inside the fire. Maybe Pele is another word for the earth's own mysterious pulse.

'OHI'A

Lava boils up from the underworld and hardens, and while it is still stone, many years before the rains have crumbled off the flakes and grains that eventually become soil, the 'ohi'a tree emerges from the rock. Its bark is gray and rough, sometimes spotted with lichen or patches of moss. The tenacious trunk will rise ten, twelve, twenty feet with no foliage, then send up a canopy of angular limbs.

It is not a pretty tree, in the way that coco palms at the shoreline can be pretty and picturesque. But it is an inspirational tree, a tree with true wilderness character, like those rams that thrive above the treeline, or like the coyote, lean and shaggy, a shrewd survivor.

Along Devastation Trail, there are trees that were stripped of all their leaves back in 1959, when the great dome-shaped cinder cone called Pu'u Puai first erupted. The ground around these trees was covered with twenty inches of pumice, which cut off their root systems from both air and water. Within a year, new leaves had sprouted. A short time later aerial roots began to appear, clumps of feeder tendrils that hang from the branches to catch moisture from the air itself.

They hang there now like thick beards, gray where they meet the limb, rusty through the center, red toward the bottom, with tiny feelers poking out, to match the 'ohi'a's anemone-like lehua blossoms, said to be Pele's flower, to match the red ohelo berry and the vein-red lava too. What a lesson in survival! With roots buried under volcanic ash, they find another way to drink and breathe.

AT THE
THRESHOLD

The water close to shore used to be azure. Lava-spewed sediment and turbulence has turned it murky green. Offshore the green is clearer, where a shallow bottom recently formed. The deepwater line is now about a hundred yards out, marked by a long sharp border where pale green meets darkest blue.

The shoreline beyond Kalapana happens to be the most southerly in the US, well below the Tropic of Cancer. At 9:30 AM it is already sultry. Near the plume the air temperature jumps about twenty degrees. The mist on the windward side is soaking me, so I swing wide around the plume for a drier and clearer view.

Lava is spilling from a tube about six feet wide and into the green-white surge. From this sizzling union the steam that churns upward becomes a tumbling cloud of purest white, rising into the bluest of all blue skies. I watch the cloud pour back against black cliffs made of last month's flow, or perhaps last night's.

The gauzy mist drifts downwind, across the plain, toward a temple site called Wahaʻula, several acres of low walls and platforms made of dark porous rock that was once hot liquid. It is one of Hawaiʻi's most sacred places, and part of Volcanoes National Park. Coco palms surround the acreage. While hiking in, I noticed that the palms nearest the ropey mounds of new *pahoe-*

hoe had become brown-leaved hulks. They had been killed not by flowing lava but by the steady fall of acid-bearing mist boiling upward from the spill.

Along this shoreline life and death intermingle, and you don't come down here to pass judgment or to wag your finger at nature's fickle and contradictory ways. You come to bear witness, to watch what happens at the planet's cutting edge.

On the way back to the car I cross a long bulging curve, the surface evidence of a tube that might be several miles long. "It starts in the hills," the geologist tells me later, "and it wanders back and forth until it finds its way to the sea. When it reaches the shore, the water will tend to cool it down and sometimes seal off the opening. So it might turn then and follow the coast," using his hands to describe these moves, and talking as if it were a willful creature cutting its serpentine path through the world.

"We have come out here with electrodes and tracked them," he says. "You try to follow the turns and the wiggles, looking for the patterns and how they work. But it's hard. You're up here. The lava is down there. Sooner or later you lose the track."

I envy these geologists. I envy their access to the rocks of the Big Island, the chance to live here and to work at this particular threshold. They are lucky, these volcano professionals. Their science and their equipment and their expertise gives them the privilege to hike out here just about any time they please, right up to the threshold of the original mystery, the creative moment, where the known and the unknown meet.

HILO

On this island, in a single day, you can see the fire that made the mountains and the curving bays. You can see trees that have sprung from the once-molten rock. Then you can see the arms of dancers become those trees, and their hands become flowers, as art and nature intertwine.

See them move out in three rows of five. Fifteen women. They wear the outfits you see in photos from the late nineteenth century—bare feet, skirts below the knee, high waist bands, long-sleeved blouses, heads crowned with ferns. The chanter begins to chant, a large Hawaiian woman loosely wrapped in one bolt of sky-blue cloth. Her voice ranges from baritone to high alto, the kind of voice that enters your bloodstream and makes your arm hairs rise with what locals call "chickenskin."

In unison, with fast precision, the fifteen women begin to move, while a drum thumps and the chanter speaks the story. Most of them are trim, but three are very heavy, thick-boned and fleshy with the weight you're not used to seeing in a dance troupe. This form of hula is not about weight. It is not about looks. It is about grace and spirit, the quality of spirit released in the dance.

And this is not the flirtatious hula you tend to see in hotel lounges. These women don't smile. They are intensely focused. In the old days it was a sacred calling. For some, it still is. I have met a couple of these women, single mothers, with kids they haul back and forth to day-care centers here in town, while they hold down low-paying jobs and find the time, at night, on weekends, to dance, to be a dancer. It is their passion and commitment, their profession, in the sense of "how you profess yourself." But there's no money in it. Like Zen novices doing practice, it is their *way*.

Later one of them will tell me how they all went up this morning into the forest to pick the ferns they've woven into the strands that circle their heads and arms. The weaving is a ritual part of the day's preparation. Together they spoke Hawaiian words to bless the dance.

"In all these gestures," she says, "you go inward and touch your center. And be aware of the earth, your feet on the earth, that is your power source."

We happen to be in Hilo, old port town and flower town on the windward side. They are warming up for the Merrie Monarch Festival, Hawai'i's most famous gathering of hula performers. It was named for David Kalakaua, the last Hawaiian king, and a man of large appetites. A great eater and drinker, he once hosted a feast for some five thousand people. He was the first ruler of any nation on earth to sail around the globe, calling on eleven heads of state from Japan to Great Britain. Among his many allies and cronies was Robert Louis Stevenson, the Scottish writer and South Seas aficionado, who visited Honolulu in 1889, ate with the king and drank his Château Lafitte, and later wrote in a letter to a friend, "He is a gentleman of courtly order and much tinctured with letters . . ."

Due to his enormous zest for life, Kalakaua came to be known as "The Merrie Monarch." But even so, and given all that, why name a dance festival for this long-gone king?

When his reign began, in 1874, traditional Hawaiian culture was dying fast. Hula had been its centerpiece, and hula had been forced underground, seldom seen at public functions. As a Hawaiian of the last century, Kalakaua was a man caught between cultures. In his official portraits he wears the uniform of a man in love with European pomp and ceremony, the epaulets and medal-laden jackets of a Prussian general. But throughout the 1870s and '80s he was writing songs and chants in his native tongue, some of which are still performed today. Grieving over the sad decline of his people and their music, he took it upon himself to revive the hula, in the face of loud protests from influential missionary families who had been trying for decades to suppress it.

The emblematic turning point was February 1883, the month of his official coronation, on the grounds of the elegant palace he had built in downtown Honolulu, called *'Iolani,* "Bird of Heaven." In front of its Italianate facade of pillars and balustrades, young island women appeared dressed in costumes made of vines and leaves. Elderly men began to beat gourd drums and chant the chants of their ancestors.

Afterward the king was attacked in private and in public. A onetime cabinet minister, W. D. Armstrong, called it a "grotesque pageantry of paganism." A Honolulu newspaper, the *Hawaiian Gazette,* described it as "the very apotheosis of grossness . . ." But with Kalakaua in command, dancing was in the open again. Hawaiian culture began to make its first comeback.

In its original form hula was narrative movement designed to enhance the meanings of the songs and chants that contained the legends, the genealogies, the stories of origins and migrations, the history of a people. It was a form of theatre and also a form of poetry, another way to acknowledge every feature of the natural world, birds and fish, trees and flowers, mountains, rivers, wind and rain, lightning, lava, steam. Kalakaua knew that if the hula died out, this old dialogue would die. The chants would die. And if the chants died, history itself might disappear.

For similar reasons hula has been central to the cultural renaissance of the past thirty years or so. At concerts and festivals you see new generations of dancers who are empowered by the reawakening of an art form that goes back a thousand years or more. With the dance has come new interest in the early drumming skills, the costume, the styles of chanting, the lyrical range of Hawaiian as it has been sung and spoken. The best of the *kumu hula* (master teachers of dance and choreography) are the bearers of an ancient flame.

❦

At the weeklong Merrie Monarch, dance troupes fly in from all the islands.

There is a royal parade down the main street in Hilo, a Miss Aloha Hula competition, days and nights of dancing in the covered pavilion called Kanaka'ole Stadium. It is named for Auntie Edith Kanaka'ole, one of the most revered and inspirational kumu hula of this century. She was born on this island and spent most of her life here, the descendent of a long and unbroken line of teachers, chanters, and dancers. Auntie Edith and the two daughters who now carry on her work trace their lineage back to Pele herself.

These festivals feature the two main forms of hula. *'Auwana,* the more undulating modern style, is usually accompanied by a three-to-five-piece Hawaiian band. In the older form, *kahiko,* each dance opens with an invocation. It may be to Kalakaua, or to Pele, or to Pele's sister, Hi'iaka, one of hula's legendary founders. Very often dancers dressed for kahiko resemble those depicted by James Webber, the documentary artist who traveled with Captain Cook on his Third Voyage to the Pacific, in the 1770s. Webber gave us the earliest pictures we have of Hawaiian life. In a typical Kahiko costume the women wear knee-length skirts of flat green ti leaves. The dark hair billows, long and full. Leis of fern encircle the heads, and fern bracelets encircle the wrists and ankles. Around the neck are draping vines or polished *kukui* nuts. The moves can be as soft as mist, or as startling as a thunder clap. Their hands talk, making fists or fluttering like leaves, telling timeless stories. The knees pop. The arms jut skyward.

They dance to the rhythm of a single drum and the insistent chanting of a single voice, sometimes male, sometimes female. It is more than a ritual speaking of words. There is a poignant squeezing of notes high in the throat, like the peak moment in flamenco or blues. That part is untranslatable, a haunting sound that slides between celebration and heartbreak. The note itself catches something that permeates the luminous air, rising from the soil, from under the soil, from the curving tunnels where lava follows its subterranean course, to tell you that all these things are of a piece, it's all one, the island platform of living rock, the pulsing voice, the 'ohi'a forest, the dancers' hands and arms becoming leaves, flowers, branches, water, roots.

BIG ISLAND
MAILROOM

At the headquarters of Volcanoes National Park, rocks arrive every day. They arrive in the mail, in packages large and small, fifty or so in an average week. They come from New Jersey, from Florida, from Hong Kong, from L.A. and Dallas and Chicago. Some are black chunks as large as a horse's head. Some are merely pebbles. Sometimes packets of black sand are sent, picked up years earlier.

They arrive in tiny cardboard boxes tightly wrapped, like jewelry. They arrive in padded envelopes shipped UPS, or Air Express. The postal charges can run to twelve, fourteen, sixteen dollars—clear evidence that some souvenir became more trouble than it was worth, and the time had come to get this out of the *house!*

Why are the rocks sent here, and sent to this particular building? According to local beliefs, if you pick up even one small shard of lava and slip it into your suitcase and carry it off, terrible things can happen. The word is *kapu*, a Hawaiian version of the more familiar Tongan word of warning, *tabu.* Since Hawai'i is Pele's island, there is a kapu on everything spewed up from the volcanoes that have formed it and continue to form it. And Halema'uma'u, her traditional home, happens to be inside the boundaries of the park.

So the mysterious and the self-evident coexist here at headquarters, which at first glance is very high-tech and up-to-date, designed to service the multitude of visitors. In the reception lobby, smoothly narrated film loops run all day long. The offices are equipped with word processors and satellite hookups. A couple of miles along the perimeter road the US Geological Survey's observation post is wired to a wall of computerized dials and screens. Around this island there are over fifty seismometers in place, and a continuous flow of signals via radio telemetry, feeding onto drum recorders and also onto magnetic tape, to be digitally recorded. Electronic tiltmeters chart ground deformation, while correlation spectrometers measure bulk sulfur dioxide emissions . . .

The most active volcanic region on earth is also the most thoroughly monitored. And yet, when you descend the stairs to the Park Service mailroom, you leave the high-tech world behind and enter another realm, where older forms of communication and energy transfer prevail. Down here, omens are in the air, signs and portents, luck both good and bad, along with the unchartable magnetisms that have sent lava rocks on a strange round-trip journey. They have traveled three and four and five thousand miles, only to be called back to their natural habitat.

I come to this mailroom out of curiosity, but not as a skeptic. The packages labeled Air Express convey an urgency I recognize. I know it all too well, since I myself have sent rocks back to this island. I have often wondered if those rocks arrived; and if so, what became of them? Now I know.

The packages and padded envelopes and boxes and letters pile up in the hallway, accumulating until Friday, when a volunteer comes in to spend most of a day opening the week's collection, to examine the contents, read the letters, then return the rocks to nearby lava fields. A rock does not have to go back to the precise spot it was taken from. But the kapu requires that it be returned to the island. Pele is a very possessive woman. According to the numerous stories and legends about her, she is also fiery, jealous, unpredictable, passionate, and vindictive.

The letters tell the story. Some are addressed to "Park Headquarters." Some are addressed to "Superintendent," or to "the Director." Some are addressed to Pele herself. Her name will appear on the envelope, as well as in the heading. The only thing I can think of that might be remotely akin to this is the annual blizzard of letters kids send to Santa Claus, hoping they will reach the North Pole in time for Christmas. But these letters are not from kids. They're from adults. They are usually typed, and rather formal. They are often detailed, full of the need to be understood, to be unburdened.

I recognize this need. I too once wrote to Pele, asking her forgiveness. Jeanne encouraged me to do it. We composed the letter together. This was some time ago, a few days after we'd returned from a family trip. When no one else was looking, our younger daughter, then eleven, had innocently picked up a Big Island souvenir to take back to her sixth-grade class. At home in Santa Cruz we set the rock on the kitchen table and looked at it.

"If we keep this," Jeanne said, "probably nothing will happen. But you hear so many stories. I think we ought to send it back."

For her such a precaution was nothing new. Where her father came from, there is a long tradition of rocks that have to be attended to. She would call it part of her inheritance, a lingering, transpacific memory of the Shinto belief in nature deities that inhabit gardens, groves, creatures, ancestral stones.

"Sending it back can't hurt anything," I said.

Pre-echoing the linguistics scholar I would meet years later, Jeanne said, "Isn't it better to be safe than sorry?"

Now I am touching this week's sheaf of pages. I touch the rocks heaped in the corridor, waiting to be hauled back to the lava fields. And I ask myself, How do you prove that something exists? In the realm of subatomic particles, it is often done by inference. *A* either occurs or does not occur, therefore *B* is probable. And so forth. The same is true for the elusive black holes at the farthest edge of observable space, and for acupuncture and verification of the meridian lines the needles are said to keep open so that vital energy can flow through.

Here in the earth and in the air and in the history of the Big Island you have this presence called Pele. She has a home, visited regularly by local residents who talk to her and leave offerings at the brink of the fire pit. I have heard chants dedicated to her, seen dances danced in her honor. I have now met people who claim to be in some way *of* her lineage, descended from her. Many claim to have seen her—sometimes as a young woman, sometimes as an aging crone—before and during eruptions. Books have been written about her, and at least one opera. And now, as visitors to this island continue to multiply, thousands of people send her things.

As I flip through this week's letters, it occurs to me that Pele is in a class by herself. Can there be another goddess, in the United States or elsewhere, with a zip code and a permanent mailing address?

> Dear Madame Pele: I am returning the lava I took from Black Sands Beach in 1969. I hope this pleases you, so my husband and I will have better luck on future trips. . . .

> Dear Madame Pele: Your volcanic rock is enclosed. There is no return address on this because I don't want any return . . .

> I hope [writes a young woman from Santa Monica] Madame Pele will understand and forgive me . . .

> Enclosed [writes a fellow from Cleveland] please find three small pieces of volcanic rock. I am not a superstitious person. However, in the last three years since I removed these from the Park, the following has occurred. . . . [His grim sequence of misfortune includes the breakup of a marriage, the loss of a home, the wreck of a brand-new car.]

> I am sending by mail my shoes [writes a fellow from West Palm Beach] worn on my trip to Hawai'i. They are dirty from the mud, which was picked up on my trip. I feel foolish doing this, but with all the bad luck I have been hearing about since my trip, you and Hawai'i can have them. I have always considered myself a lucky person. But in the six to eight weeks after leaving Hawai'i I have heard over thirty separate incidents of bad luck. It's unreal. A former native of Hawai'i sincerely told me to send the shoes back.

Dear Park Superintendent: Please entreat her to release us
from her terrible spell . . .

Is it possible that chunks and bits of once-molten lava can actually carry
ancient signals thousands of miles across the water? Reason of course says,
No, a rock is a rock, and the rest is hocus-pocus. Yet the volume of mail, when
you see it heaped here, is very impressive, not easy to dismiss. Fifty packages
in an average week adds up to twenty-five hundred or so in an average year—
from people in faraway urban centers who live by the laws of concrete and
spreadsheets and who, if pressed, would probably claim to know better:

I feel foolish doing this, but . . .

I am not a superstitious person, however . . .

Maybe it's superstition. Maybe it's a collective hallucination. Maybe it's a
form of recognition. Behind the kapu is a Hawaiian reverence for their extraordinary island terrain. What the kapu tells us is that these rocks have a natural place in the world, and maybe that's where they would like to remain.

FIRE IN
THE NIGHT

Among volcano buffs there is a little rite of passage whereby you stick your hand ax into moving lava and bring away a gob of the molten stuff. In order to do this you have to be where the lava is flowing and hot. Then you have to get your body in close enough to reach down toward the edge of the flow. And it usually means you have to walk or stand at least a few seconds on some pretty thin crust.

My chance came one night last week. I was traveling in the company of Jack Lockwood, a specialist in volcanic hazards with the US Geological Survey. He is a trim and wiry fellow, with wild hair and a devilish grin, a man from New England who has found this island, its craters and flows, to be his natural habitat. He loves it here, he loves the smoothly folded look of the lava called *pahoehoe,* the many shapes it takes. He will stop the car to study the way today's flow has poured over yesterday's, making a drapery of knobs and drips. He will remark upon the metallic sheen in the late sun, and then point out that newer lava can be crumbled with your shoe, while the stuff that came through yesterday has already hardened under a rainfall and thus is firmer.

We park where the yellow line of the coast road disappears under a ten-foot wall of new rock. We get out the packs, the gloves, the canteens, the flashlights, the hard hats. Jack's hat is custom-made, with his name in raised letters on the metal. His hard-toe boots are scuffed ragged with threads of rock-torn leather. I was going to wear running shoes for this expedition, until he told me no. "Where we're going," he said while we were packing, "the soles could peel right off."

Hunkered on the asphalt, lacing up the high-top boots I've borrowed, I can already feel it shimmering toward us. Minutes later we are hiking through furnace heat, over lava that has rolled across here just a few hours ago. Through cracks and fissures you can see the molten underlayer showing, three or four inches below the dark surface.

"You can actually walk on it fifteen or twenty minutes after it starts to harden," Jack says, "as long as you have an inch of surface underfoot."

Soon the red slits are everywhere, and we're crossing what appears to be several acres of recent flow. Jack plunges ahead with great purpose, with long firm strides, planting each foot and leaning forward as he walks, as if there is a path to be followed and we are on it—though of course there is no path, no prior footprints, no markers of any kind to guide us across terrain that wasn't here this morning.

"Jack," I say, "have you ever stepped into a soft spot? I mean, got burned, fallen through?"

He shakes his head vigorously. "Nope."

"How do you know where to step?"

He stops and looks at me with his mischievous eyes, his beard and squint reminding me of a young John Huston. "You just pick your way and pay attention as you go. It's partly experience and partly faith."

"Faith?"

"You have to put your trust in Pele. Tell her you come out here with respect, and she'll take care of you."

As he plunges on, I want to trust in Pele, whose crater/home is about fifteen miles upslope from where we're walking. We have already talked about her, while driving down Chain of Craters Road, and I know he means what he just said. But I have to confess that at the moment I am putting my full trust in Lockwood, placing my feet where he places his, stepping in his steps as we stride and leap from rock to rock.

Eventually the heat subsides, and we're hiking over cooler stuff, though none of it is very old.

"Everything you see has flowed through in the last six months," he says.

Two-and-a-half miles of the coast road have recently been covered, as well as the old settlement of Kamoamoa, near where we parked. Inland we can see some of what remains of Royal Gardens, a subdivision laid out in the early 1970s, laid right across a slope of the East Rift Zone. In the Royal Gardens grid, cross-streets were named for tropical flowers—Gardenia, Pikake—while the broader main streets sound noble—Kamehameha, Prince. I have been up there. You have to be careful when you turn a corner. Take a left and you are liable to come upon a charcoal heap the size of a football field, with a fallen street sign poking through to remind you that this had been the intersection where Ali'i Drive met Plumeria Boulevard, where homebound motorists once slowed down to look both ways before crossing.

From the shoreline now, it looks as if great vats of black paint have been dumped over the highest ridge, to pour down the slope and through the trees, to cover lawns and long-lost driveways.

Our destination—the spilling end of another lava tube—is marked by a steam plume rising high against the evening sky. When we left the car it was white and feathery at the top, two miles down the coast. After the sun has set and the light begins to dim, the plume turns pink and red. Spatter thrown up from the collision of lava and surf has formed a littoral cone now outlined against the steam. As we approach, tiny figures can be seen standing at the edge of this cone, like cutouts against the fiery backdrop.

On one side of the cone, flat spreads of lava ooze toward the cliff. On the other side, an orange gusher is arcing thirty feet above the water, while a mound slowly rises beneath it. Beyond this tube, another spill obscured by steam sends lava straight into the water at about sea level. Black and crimson floating gobs spew out from the steam, or sometimes fly into the air, breaking into fiery spatter that is gradually building the littoral cone.

These fires light the billowing plume from below. As it churns away toward the west, it sends a pinkish glow back down onto the marbled surf, which makes me think of the Royal Hawaiian Hotel, where they spend a lot of money on lightbulbs and filters trying to tint the offshore waters a Waikiki pink that can never come close to Pele's cosmetic kit.

A video cameraman is out here, perched at the cliff edge, filming the buildup on the mound below the arching orange tube. His tripod legs are spindly black against the glow. Nearby a couple of dozen people from Volcano Observatory and the University of Hawai'i stand gazing at the spectacle. They are out here in numbers, Jack tells me later, because this is a rare night. Spills like this are usually closer to the surf, and the lava will pour until the mound builds from below to seal off its opening. But this littoral cone is unstable, and part of it has fallen away, to behead the end of the tube, so the lava spills free from high up the cliff, making an endless column of liquid orange.

If you can take your eyes off its mesmerizing arc and turn inland, you can see another glow in the night. It hangs above the nearest ridge, light from the lake called Kupaianaha, the source of the lava moving around us. It's a new lake, inside a new shield cone. From there the lava snakes seaward via a channel that loops wide to the east, then back toward where we stand. You can see evidence of its twisting, subterranean path about halfway down the mountain, where tiny fires seem to be burning, four or five eyes of flame against the black.

We linger for an hour, maybe more, chatting, bearing witness, sharing our wonder with the others lucky enough to be out here on such a night, at the cutting edge of destruction and creation. We are about to start back when Lockwood says this is probably as good a time as any for me to add my name to the "one thousandth of one percent of the human population who have stuck their ax in hot lava." And with that he begins to prowl around a couple of oozing streams, to see how close we can get.

I watch him step out onto some hot stuff that has barely stopped moving, and see the surface give under his boot. With a grin he jumps back. "That's probably a little too soft."

We move around to the far side, forty feet away, and approach the fiery mush from another angle. With ax in hand he hops across the one-inch crust and digs into the front edge of a narrow strip, but it's already cooling and a little too thick to lift. He can only pull it up an inch or so, the front lip already in that halfway zone between liquid and solid stone.

He's pulling so hard he loses his footing and half falls toward the crust. His gloved hand reaches out to take the fall. For a moment his crouching body is silhouetted against the molten stream, while behind him the red and orange steam plume surges like a backdrop curtain for his dance. He comes rolling and hopping toward me with a wild grin and a rascal eye.

"That's a little too viscous. It's surprising. It's cooler than it looks."

So we move on, heading back the way we've come, under a black sky with its infinity of stars, our flashlight beams bobbing across the rocks, while the plume grows smaller behind us.

We drop down to a new beach of dark volcanic sand, then climb out of the sand onto that day's fresh lava, where the red slits once again glow around us. As we pick our way, in the furnace heat, we come upon a flow that wasn't here when we crossed the first time.

"Pele is being good to you," says Jack, grinning, his beard red-tinted underneath. He hands me his ax. "This is perfect. Just keep your back to the heat, and move in quickly."

Which is what I do.

The stream is maybe twenty feet wide, crackling, creeping toward the sea. I backpedal up next to it, reaching with the flat chisel-end of the metal blade, dip and scoop into the burning lip. It is smoother than wet cement, thicker than honey, thicker than three-finger poi. Maybe the consistency of glazing compound, or the wet clay potters use. For the first mini-second it feels that way. As I dig in and pull, it is already harder. It clings to the flow, but I tug and finally come away with a chunk the size of a tennis ball, which holds to the blade as I leap back away from the heat.

Jack is excited. "Throw it down here, quickly!"

I plop it between us, on a black slab.

"Now press your heel in hard!"

I press my boot heel into the glob, flattening it with a bootprint. When the rubber begins to smoke, I pull my foot away.

"Now," he says, with a happy grin, "we'll put this on my shovel blade and carry it to the car while it cools, and this will be your souvenir."

By the time we reach the asphalt road, the heat has given way to balmy coastal air off the water. The slits and fissures and plumes and flows are all behind us, and that is the end of our expedition.

But it is not the end of my relationship with this flattened piece of rock. I live with it for another week, trying to decide what to do. After such a magical night, the idea of a souvenir appeals to me. It is mine, I suppose, because I have marked it with my boot. It is smooth, as shiny as black glass, and if I lived here I'd probably have it sitting on my desk for years. But I don't feel right about bringing this trophy back home. I keep thinking about the tug of the lava as I pulled the ax away. Through the handle I felt its texture, its consistency, and something else that haunts me. A reluctance. A protest. As if live flesh were being torn from a body.

Maybe this is what the Hawaiians mean when they say all the rocks belong to Pele and should not leave the island. Maybe the unwritten law that says Be respectful of the rocks is another way of honoring that old yearning in the stone. Maybe I have finally understood something, through my hands, something I've heard about and read about and talked about and even tried to write about.

❦

A couple of days ago I drove down to the south shore again. Sighting from the new black sand beach I think I got pretty close to where we'd been. I dropped the chunk of lava down into a jagged crevice and asked it to forgive me for any liberties I might have taken, and I thanked Pele for letting me carry this rock around for a while.

Back on the mainland I probably won't tell anybody about this. You come home and tell someone you've been talking to rocks, they give you that certain kind of look. I've mentioned it to Jack Lockwood, of course. It's easier to talk about when you're here in the islands. When you're in or near volcano country, it's easier to remember that each rock was once a moving, breathing thing, as red as blood and making eyes of fire in the night.

KEALAKEKUA

Here is where the ships dropped anchor in January 1779, the sparkling bay, as blue as the blue in the Union Jack, the long descending ridge. Here is the very scene you see in James Webber's oft-reprinted etching from Cook's third voyage, "A View of Karakakooa in Owyhee." Its backdrop is a triangular slope of stone and brush that is still here, much as it appeared to Webber, as he sketched the ships standing offshore, the *Resolution* and the *Discovery,* surrounded by swimmers and canoes. He must have stood just about where I am standing, on the Napo'pop'o side of this little bay, site of the famous flashpoint, symbolic clash of cultures.

This island's leeward shore is loaded with Pacific history. At the time of Cook's arrival, it was the most populous region of all the islands. There were dozens of communities, hundreds of temples and sacred places. Up at the northern end, near 'Upolu Point, is the birthplace of Kamehameha I. At Kailua, once the king's royal town and still the main town on this side, the first missionaries from New England landed in 1821 and built a church, to launch what has been called the world's most successful Christianizing campaign. A few years later they built a larger church, which burned, so they built a third, which still stands, its white steeple rising out of coco palms, its ceiling supported by two rows of perfectly straight 'ohi'a logs hauled down out of the high forest, its walls made of mortared lava blocks.

Around here everything is made of lava, fence lines, house foundations,

Hawai'i's first Christian church, and the old temple where James Cook was deified. That's still here too. *Hikiau heiau* fronts on the bay, a cleared platform of porous black stone, about the size of a tennis court. Here Cook was honored as a high chief with divine powers, perhaps a reincarnation of Lono, the god of peace, prosperity and agriculture.

The place-name, *Kealakekua,* happens to mean "pathway of the god."

When they ushered him up onto this platform, the carved wooden deity figures were still in place, and the spindly oracle tower. They covered him with vines and honors, chants and blessings. Less than a month later they clubbed him and stabbed him to death. They stripped the flesh from his bones and disposed of his remains in ways that are mysterious to this day. I've heard local people say his bones are still on this island, somewhere up inside a lava tube whose opening was concealed and will never be found.

A white obelisk marks the spot where Cook was slain. I can see it over there across the water, at the foot of that long descending ridge, almost inaccessible by car, they say, but often visited by tour boats that motor down from the hotels.

It brings to mind another monument I saw not long ago, in the Philippines, where Ferdinand Magellan landed in 1521 and where he too was killed. On the island of Mactan, near Cebu, about two hundred and fifty miles south of Manila, a statue marks the spot. The big difference between Mactan and Kealakekua is that the marker there does not memorialize the slain European, it honors the fellow who did him in, a local chief named Lapu Lapu.

The bronze figure, about twelve feet high, is broad shouldered, in loincloth, with a spear, depicted as a noble tribesman overlooking what is now a swampy tide flat. The plaque describes him as the first Filipino to resist European imperialist expansion. He is still a hero, and a very tasty local fish bears his name.

On the seas of history Magellan and Cook were the great explorers of their eras, navigators, pathfinders. They drew long lines across the empty water. Towns and islands and straits have been named for them. But in hindsight, knowing what we now know about the fates of indigenous peoples everywhere, can you fault the warriors and chiefs for an urge to draw the line on these potent foreigners who suddenly appeared with ships so large the Hawaiians called them "floating islands"? These twin responses to Cook and his men seem to sum it all up: an initial awe and wonder, followed four weeks later by the desire to kill and bury.

Numerous historians have analyzed those weeks. Had the British overstayed their welcome? Had they offended too many people in too short a time? They had had their way with many women. They had defiled temple sites. The Hawaiians meanwhile were stealing nails and knives and anything else made of iron. The sailors were running out of patience. Cook himself was on a short fuse, by this point in his third voyage into parts unknown and semiknown, more punitive toward his own men than the legendary Captain Bligh would be a few years later, more brutal in his punishments. In two other archipelagoes, other islanders had recently tried to take Cook's life.

It came to a head one February morning on the shores of this quietly gorgeous curve of coastline, where a thousand Hawaiians had gathered, after news spread that Cook had tried to abduct their king and hold him hostage, in retaliation for the theft of a longboat. The most vivid account is still the first, as recorded by Cook's lieutenant, James King, who witnessed the events:

> Whilst he faced the natives none of them had offered him any violence, but having turned about to give his orders to the boats he was stabbed in the back, and fell with his face into the water. On seeing him fall the islanders set up a great shout, and his body was immediately dragged on shore and surrounded by the enemy, who, snatching the dagger out of each other's hands, showed a savage eagerness to have a share in his destruction. Thus fell our great and excellent commander![4]

The Hawaiians had no written language for keeping records of events like this. But they had a long oral tradition of lyric and narrative poetry. It was a high calling, and one thing a poet did was respond to recent events, love affairs, births and deaths, voyages and battles.

On the Big Island, in those days, there was a well-known poet who had seen the British and their ships. He had heard the unfamiliar roar of their cannons and seen some of his fellow islanders fall before the musket blast. Here was a new and formidable kind of power that foretold great changes for his world. The question he seemed to ask himself was, How do we prepare ourselves to deal with such power and such a challenge?

His name was Ke'aulumoku. An ally of Kamehameha, he had come of age long before Cook's arrival, and he lived until 1784. He was a chief, a chanter, a singer, a visionary. After those ships departed, he composed a chant, which makes its point in a line that says, "Hold on to your land."[5]

This did not mean, "Hold on to the deed to your property so these foreigners can't steal it away from you." Hawaiians did not yet know such things were possible. Though your family may have inhabited a place for centuries, this did not include the idea of property that could be lost, or owned as a commodity to be bought and sold. Ke'aulumoku was saying "Hold on," in the sense that your mother tells you to "hold on to your brother's hand while you're crossing the street." Or, "Hold on for dear life!"

According to my friend, John Charlot, at the University of Hawai'i, who reads the language, and who has studied and translated this poem, the line can also be read to mean, "Be held by your land."

Challenged and troubled by the British and their ships, the poet asks himself, Who are these strangers? How do they think? When will they be back? And what does this mean for our people? His response is to look within and try to voice what it means to be a person of these islands, to find the essential touchpoint. In this two-hundred-year-old poem he expresses an idea that is heard and felt again today, with ever more vigor and passion—though maybe *idea* is the wrong word. It is a form of relationship, and it has been central to the cultural revival. It is also central to the Hawaiian sovereignty movement: Be held by the land, which is your anchor and ground wire, as well as your way of knowing the higher power. Through the land and your connections with it, you find your truest strength.

According to my friend Charlot, this old poet's name, *Ke'aulumoku,* means "the lava that makes the land grow."

MO'OKINI

Mo'okini is out here by itself, a mound of stones on a treeless point. No coco palms for shade, no white beaches, no condos overlooking the turquoise pool. The dirt road is iron red. It leads you through two miles of cane field to a broad clearing and a long rectangle of lichen-spotted chunks of lava. Inside the sloping walls there are pathways and restored stone platforms open to the sky.

It is said to be among the most venerable and revered of all Hawaiian places—the walled worship site, nearly the size of a soccer field, as well as the surrounding terrain. Members of the Mo'okini family have been the appointed guardians of this site for over fifteen hundred years. According to their genealogical chant, the *heiau* dates back farther than Taos Pueblo, farther than the temples of the sun and moon at Teotihuacan.

It was first laid out in 480 AD, under the direction of Kuamo'o Mo'okini, the high priest from whom all guardians have descended. The walls were originally six feet high. About a thousand years ago the temple was enlarged by a priest from Samoa, named *Pa'ao*. The walls were raised to their present height of thirty feet, without the use of mortar, and a unique scalloped altar was added inside. A family chant tells us the new stones came from Pololu Valley, fourteen miles down the coast toward Hilo. They were moved in a single night. Between sunset and sunrise, fifteen thousand men stood in a line and passed the stones by hand, from the deep valley to this windswept headland.

I have heard of Moʻokini for years. I have seen photos of the ancient stones where the birth of Kamehameha I was consecrated (he was born just a thousand yards away). I have read about the long stewardship of the Moʻokini family. What I did not know, could never have grasped from afar, or by reading, or by studying all the photographs, was the impact of the location.

Moʻokini occupies the very end of the Big Island's northernmost point, a peninsula that juts like a thumb, pointing across the channel toward Maui. Standing here you have behind you the green and rugged slopes of the Kohala Range, and in front of you, Maui's high shield cone, Haleakala. It is the world's largest dormant volcano. Viewed from the south, it is noble, blood-stirring, rising straight out of the sea.

Wind through the channel is constant and as eerie as the silence of the craters, while the waters are spectacularly blue, a moving, shifting, current-driven blue. The point is empty. The sea is moving. Twenty-five miles across the channel the old volcano, in early afternoon, makes a dark cone against the sky.

It is the kind of place you have to react to. You have to mark the spot, or write about it in your journal. Standing here, it isn't hard to imagine the first human who stopped and gazed toward the next island in the constant wind and felt an urge to consecrate the moment, to send a voice across the water, make a song or a chant or gather a few stones in a heap, as a way of saying, "I touched this place, and the place touched me."

Perhaps that first visitor tells others a story that includes something about the look and feel of the barren point, and this story conveys whatever it called out of him. Eventually someone else wants to see what he is talking about and comes and stands and adds a stone to the pile or sends another call across the channel. And there is an agreement that, yes, the place has a kind of power, which is to say, it releases something in those who experience it. Nowadays we might name this reverence, or wonder, or awe.

I believe such feelings can linger in the air and in the land, gathering over time, in invisible layers. After enough people have visited a spot, to stand, to pray, to sing, to fast, to chant, century upon century, its original impact has been layered and amplified until the ancestral atmosphere around a site like this one is so rich with what Hawaiians call *mana* you can feel it like a coating on your skin.

The atmosphere seems denser here, thick with its own history of reaching toward the higher power. Though I am not Hawaiian and can claim no ties to this temple's long tradition, I feel profoundly connected to the place. During the couple of hours I wander inside and outside the rocky walls, I feel I'm in a state of grace.

Trying to explain this to myself, I begin to think of sacredness as a kind of dialogue between the human spirit and certain designated places. These sites that call forth reverence and awe and humility and wonder, we make them sacred. It is a way of honoring those feelings in ourselves. And when we hear the songs the places sing, we are hearing our own most ancient voices.

I believe there is a place in each of us where the entire universe resides, and it includes these rocks at Mo'okini, as well as the craters that produce them. I have been living on this island a month now. Lava rocks, large and small, are everywhere—marking property lines, in the numerous temple remains, in all the legends. You can touch rocks no one dares to move, and you can touch some of the newest rocks on earth. In this world of moving stone, it occurs to me that we have all been lava once, and that those ties are never lost. They may be forgotten. But they are not lost.

During these weeks I have been eating produce grown right here—papayas, bananas, mangoes, cucumber, onions. And where do all these local fruits and vegetables get their nutrients?

From the soil, of course.

And where does the soil come from?

It too started out as lava belched up from Kilauea and Mauna Loa and Mauna Kea and Hualalai, to be broken down by millennia of rain and wind.

Am I then that much different from the shaggy 'ohi'a tree, which feeds off the rock and is the stubborn dancer anchored to the lava slopes and old volcanic mountainsides?

These nutrients taken from produce grown in soil that began as molten lava, they are now somewhere in my bloodstream, entering my cells. Multiply that, I tell myself, by four billion years or so, by all the recycled incarnations of all the bits of matter I'm composed of, and isn't there going to be a chorus of voices to be listened to, called forth, released?

A month on the Big Island has made it clear that I have things in common with the stones first gathered at Mo'okini heiau fifteen hundred years ago. Though they may be forgotten, these ancient ties are never lost. In the presence of the stones they come whispering, the oldest voices, calling from within.

THREE KINDS
OF SILENCE

Kilauea-iki is a companion crater to the great caldera (*iki* meaning small, the smaller version). On my last day here, I hike out across this flat-bottomed bowl of steam and foggy mist, and it brings to mind a Zen garden we saw not long ago in the old temple town of Dazaifu, once the principal city of Kyushu. Listening to the silence of the crater, I finally understand the silence of that garden. It is the difference between the ripples made by a rock dropped into a pond, and the pond itself.

Kilauea-iki is about half a mile wide, an amphitheater of undulating stone, fractured, with hut-size chunks emerging. Though the crust you walk on has been hard for years, it's still molten down below. Steam rises everywhere, through dozens of vents and fissures, filling the air with wispy banners. While you're inside this crater you feel the bowl of it, shaped like a deeply-tiered stadium, like Stanford Stadium with all seats empty, its steep sides lined with 'ohi'a trees. In volcano country you measure age by the size of the 'ohi'a. In the most recent flows, tiny sprouts are poking through the cracks. On older slopes you find shaggy trunks three and four feet thick.

On these walls the trunks are slender, saplings, growing close together, among huge ferns called hapu'u. You cross this bleak half mile of raw lava bed, with the vents seething, and step right into a tropical forest, where ground ferns climb the slopes. Over the small ferns, the high and pale-green hapuʻu arch twenty-five and thirty feet. Halfway up the trail I stop, where a wide portal through fern and ʻohiʻa branches gives me a fine view of the terrain I've just crossed. Sheets of feathery mist drift into the crater, under a sky that would be somber if it ever stopped moving. But the sky is never still, always opening, closing, opening again.

A sheet of mist.

A blue window above the mist.

The lava is black and gray and chalked with white. Along the walls there are rusty streaks. It is harsh, unforgiving, the roughest kind of primal rock. You wouldn't want to be caught overnight in such a place. And yet it is contained, with narrow, cairn-marked paths leading into and out of the bowl, so it is observable, and somehow manageable, like an aquarium where sharks and barracuda prowl.

It looks ancient, yet it is one of the world's newer places, having taken its present form and look as recently as 1959, when all of this belched out from the vent of what is now called *Puʻu Puaʻi*. (*Puʻu* means hill; *puaʻi* means flow or bubble or boil.) The bowl filled with four hundred feet of new lava, which has subsided some, leaving a bathtub ring. Fire columns spouted nineteen hundred feet, over a quarter mile straight up. That kind of energy, that contained pressure and the memory of explosive release is what hovers in the air and just below the surface, mixing with the mist.

It makes the silence potent. Though the earth seems still, nothing is at rest.

Dazaifu is thirty minutes south of Fukuoka, by train. Established in the seventh century, it was once the region's capitol and one of the more prominent cities in southern Japan. Now it's famous for its shrines and temples. Once in fall and once in winter, Jeanne and I rode out there.

The first time, we went looking for the main attraction, a large and elaborate Shinto shrine—gold leaf, red pillars, the entry roofed like a warrior's helmet. It is dedicated to Sugawara Michizane, the mortal man and revered leader who was later deified. Among other things he is known as the god of studies, so the courtyard is always packed with classes of uniformed school kids who arrive by train and bus, class after class, marching in two by two to buy good luck amulets from the many booths around the central courtyard, amulets to bless the next exam, or to bless the course of study, or to bless the general aptitude and long-term success. They bunch close to the barrier set up in front of the stairs that lead to the altar, where you clap your hands twice, bow your head to offer up your silent prayer, then throw a coin or two toward the stairs.

It was very busy in there, in the courtyard of the Shinto shrine at Dazaifu, with hands clapping, and cameras clicking, and two or three hundred visitors milling around. Jeanne and I were much relieved to wander down a side street for a couple of blocks and come upon the Zen temple called Komyoji, considerably smaller and seldom visited, the lines simpler, the wooden buildings unpainted. In front, next to the road, nine stones rise out of gravel raked in curves and circles, the kind of rock garden that conveys the sense of islands in the sea.

Behind the buildings there is another garden, hidden from the road. The second time we made this trip, winter had stripped the trees. The first time we stood on the shaded wooden porch, the inner garden was subtly brilliant with the colors of autumn, slender trunks, leaves of lime green and darker green, yellow and rust and russet leaves in layers and canopies over stones and mosses in their lakes of contoured gravel.

A steep hillside rises up behind the garden, adding more layers of foliage, bamboo and pine, creating the illusion of an endless forest. There is never any wind. The serenity of the place is perfect. It has been perfected. The silence has been eloquently sculpted, shaped by humans, to acknowledge the absolute, giving the garden the quality of a fine poem or a fine novel or piece of music, another version of the dialogue between the mind and whatever you want to call the vast and all-surrounding presence we move through, as it moves through us.

At Kilauea-iki steam comes rising through the scorched rock twenty-four hours a day, every day of the year, whether or not anyone watches or cares. The rocks move of their own volition, whenever they are ready to move. The waiting, loaded silence that pervades the place is outside any time or season.

At Komyoji temple, you stand in awe of what man can do with the ingredients of nature, the immaculate managing of space and foliage. You admire the reverent attentiveness of the gardener, as much as you admire the trees, the rocks, the shrubs. The gardener has had a hand in the quality of that silence.

❧

When the mist clears, the late sun's shadow moves along the broken floor. Then the bowl is all in shadow, as cloud cover crosses the sky. I climb the zigzag trail to the rim and look back. What was cloud cover lower down becomes misty fog, shreds of gauzy curtain that give me intermittent glimpses of the flat-floored bowl. From the rim I can't tell which is shredding fog and which is steam seeping from distant cracks.

Half a mile along the rim, then through a long 'ohi'a grove, and I come out near the brink of Kilauea, its farther side in deep shadow, after the sun drops. Soon I am standing at the vista point called Waldron Ledge, looking west at a silver sky that makes the vast caldera blacker than black, while the light itself tints steam plumes wavering against the void.

After I have gazed a while across this burnt and monumental terrain, I find myself wondering, again, how it is possible for an empty dish of rocks, dark lava, misty plumes to command one's full attention. What do such places speak to? In their silence what do we hear? Why is primal landscape so compelling?

Is this the kinship that runs deeper than all others, deeper than family or clan or nation or culture? Yes. Of course. The sense of wonder comes from being reminded of something profound you have almost forgotten. This is the point of origin. This is the source. The Polynesians knew it. The Apache knew it. The Lakota Sioux. The Wintu. The Miwok. We all knew it. Once. We city-bound and media-dazed, our tribes knew it too, many centuries ago, and now, in this crisis time of spiritual yearning we gradually begin to remember where we all have come from. In these mirrors we remember our oldest selves.

The rocks are us. The peaks are us, the bluffs, the canyons, the coves, the plains, ancestors sprung from the same stuff, the original stuff. Old old tribal memories come surfacing as "an aesthetic." Raw nature, we generally agree, is pleasing to behold. We call it "scenery." Standing at the vista point, we gaze. The tears well up. The chest fills with unvoicable feeling. What are you gazing at?

Ancestral portraits. Pictures of home.

Another cloud has filled the sky. The light grows somehow larger, brighter, moving in underneath this cloud. Unaware of sound, I am watching the light, watch until the west turns red-maroon, while overhead half a moon breaks through, making shadows on the cliff where I stand. I watch the near-night colors merge and change until a white spirit comes rising from somewhere farther down the precipice, right below me. Huge white wings are lifting in slow undulation. It is a white owl, the one Hawaiians call *pueo*, top-lit by the moon. With a feathery whoosh it swings wide, and behind that whoosh comes the non-sound of its sudden passage, a silence with a shape to it, like the dark blur the owl leaves on my retina, rising, curving, swooping, gone.

WHERE THE TWO WORLDS TOUCH

III

UBUD, DENPASAR, KUTA BEACH, JAKARTA

The breeze at dawn has secrets to tell you.
    Don't go back to sleep.
You must ask for what you really want.
    Don't go back to sleep.
People are going back and forth across the doorsill
    where the two worlds touch.
The door is round and open.
    Don't go back to sleep.
           —Jelaluddin Rumi, (1207–1273)

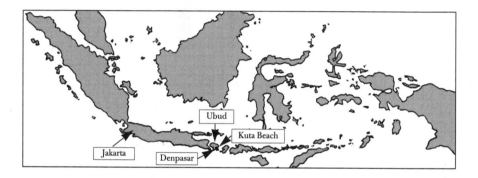

Indonesia. To the north: Malaysia, the Philippines; to the east: Papua New Guinea; to the west: the Indian Ocean; to the south: Australia.

TECTONIC
LINES AND
FAMILY LINES

On Maui there is Haleakala. On Honshu there is Fujiyama. Up north of here, the high cone of Mount Shasta changes color as you approach, and it's no mystery at all why such peaks—singular, triangular, and wondrous—should be endowed with the power to nurture, to guide, to heal.

Not long ago we were driving home from Oregon on Highway Five, watching Shasta grow ahead of us. From fifty miles away the slopes appeared to be smoky blue, rising against the palest of pale blue skies. Below the peak, crevices and canyons were streaked with snow in mid-July. By the time we'd passed through downtown Weed the great mountain was ten miles away, and the lower slopes were green with grasses, darkened by groves thinning out at the tree line. Above that the higher slopes were the color of light milk chocolate, with flat drapes of patchy snow below the bare and jagged topmost ridge.

Minutes later, from due west, in a full midafternoon sun, the upper reaches had the same coloring as Mauna Kea's, a mauve-tinted sandy tan. Near the highway stood a cinder cone, gray with graveled rock thrown out how long ago? It has been two hundred years since the last eruption, they say, long enough for trees to rise from the cinder slopes, and fall, and rise again.

Shasta and Lassen are at the lower end of the Cascade chain that stretches from California north into Oregon, across central Washington, from Mount Mazama (which exploded to become the bowl called Crater Lake) and Mount Hood, to Mount Adams, Mount St. Helens, Mount Rainier, and Glacier Peak, with Mount Baker looming close to Canada. This long archipelago of western peaks and craters follows the continental curve, some alive, some extinct, some dormant, waiting, always waiting, like Shasta, where springs simmer near the top. Imagine water rising from the subterranean stove up to fourteen thousand feet or so. Kettle water.

I recently talked with a fellow who knows that mountain inside and out. His name is Frank La Pena, stocky and brown-skinned, with a silver beard and silver hair receding from a smooth forehead. He heads the Native American Studies program at Sacramento State University. He grew up farther north, near the McCloud River, a region that is traditionally the home territory of his people, the Wintu. They have called it home for over ten thousand years.

Frank is a man so deeply rooted you can almost think the western earth speaks through him. He likes to talk about Shasta, which dominates the landscape in Wintu country. For him it's much more than a dramatic peak and photographer's delight, much more than a challenge for climbers and skiers. For him the mountain is a mentor, it's a holy place he approaches with reverence.

"If you sit still and listen to it," he said quietly, "it can tell you a lot."

He described a sacred spring, one you reach via an old trail not marked on any map. "I used to get water there to take as a gift to my uncle, who was an elder on the Clear Creek Reservation. It was the best gift I could take him, because he knew where it came from, that it came from the mountain and was blessed. You have different kinds of springs up there, you see. Some are sulfur. Some are hot. This was a soda spring, with cleansing and purifying properties. You offer a prayer when you take the water. And all this would be carried in the jar I brought to my uncle."

Heaped with generations of family memory, Shasta also serves as a chapel and a sanctuary. He talked about a pilgrimage he once made to the mountain when another uncle passed away. Frank went on foot and left behind a lock of his own hair, as he expressed his grief and prayed for his uncle's safe passage. For the Wintu, who call themselves "the mountain/river people," Shasta is your final point of contact with this world, and your gateway to the next.

As I heard Frank's stories I envied him, and I told him so. I told him that after the Loma Prieta Quake back in October 1989, with its epicenter just eight

*miles from where we live, here in Santa Cruz, after the long, rolling earth wave
had come and gone, after all the shaking had subsided, I continued to shake
within. I told him that perhaps I had begun to understand then why
Hawaiians had recognized Hale-maʻumaʻu as a place where offerings could be
left and prayers could be spoken. I told him that I too longed for a place I could
go to and stand and voice my fear and release my anxiety and make some kind
of peace with the powers that inhabit the earth. I was born in San Francisco,
I told him, had lived almost all my life in earthquake country, never more than
a few miles from the crease called the San Andreas Fault, which cuts its long
path from Cape Mendocino south to the Sea of Cortez. "And yet, as you tell me
about your pilgrimage to the mountain, I realize what a yearning I have for
that kind of ritual, for that kind of relationship. I wish my culture provided me
with more guidance in this area. But it doesn't . . ."*

I was astounded by his reply.

*"You don't have to deprive yourself of that," Frank said. "It is really up to
you. It is always available. You can awaken this aspect of a place, if you make
your own connection with it."*

It is really up to you!

*Here was a truly liberating idea—that I could awaken the sacred aspect of
a place, or at least open the way to that possibility. You don't have to be a Wintu
with ten thousand years in residence, he was saying. Be awakened to these
places in yourself, he was saying. That is where it starts.*

❧

*I needed to hear this lesson. In ways I would later understand, it prepared me
for a trip I was about to take, to the Indonesian island of Bali, where there is
also a shield cone that dominates the terrain. Mount Agung is a dormant volcano that last erupted in 1963. On Bali it is a continuous reference point,
scenic, inspirational, cultural. People there acknowledge it every day in a
dozen ways. They bow toward it. They position altars with the mountain in
mind. They point their beds in that direction. Besakih, the Mother Temple, the
island's largest place of worship, is built high upon the flank of Mount Agung.*

Later on it would occur to me that something about Frank himself seemed to be in close harmony with the Balinese way. It is one of those resemblances that starts you pondering the often talked-about link between certain Asian peoples and the indigenous tribes of the Americas. It is not only his brown skin and penetrator eyes and gentleness of speech; it is his quality of spirit, his undisguised reverential manner, his readiness to acknowledge the sacred dimension in the forms of nature. Amid the hectic swirl of late-twentieth-century California, he continues to inhabit a world where geology and the spiritual path and daily life converge.

AT DEVI SRI

At Devi Sri the tiny restaurant is an open-air pavilion floored with red tile. The thatch roof is raised on straight wooden legs. There are five tables. Beyond the tables, beyond the carp pool, you have a view across rice fields toward other thatch roofs among the palms that line Monkey Forest Road. Very close to where I sit sipping my coffee, a family shrine is wrapped with the cloth of black and white checks that represent the eternal struggle between good and evil. And over in the corner I see a twelve-foot Garuda, the feathered bird-man who is Bali's totem figure of transcendence—knees bent, eagle-face, wings spread and rising green and red and gold.

This is the amazing thing: coffee, papaya, the television screen, and a deity figure, all together in the same place. Imagine sitting in the United States in a restaurant decorated with the twelve stages of the cross, ham and eggs next to an altar flickering with votive candles. Would diners find it appropriate? Would you sell much food? Probably not. In the US the realm of the spirit is one thing. Breakfast is something else. Not so in Bali, where this row of rental bungalows is named for the rice goddess, where Garuda presides over your banana fritter, where the mask-dancer goes into the temple to bless his masks and consecrate the dance before he steps back out into the courtyard to depict The Prime Minister, The Clown, The King.

TRAVELING
WITH A HINDU

So much depends on who you're with. Two years ago I flew in for a conference at one of the beach hotels. Most of what I saw then was a big resort, somewhere between Palm Springs and the leeward shore of Maui, with a low-budget marketplace thrown in for great deals on woven baskets and local shirts.

This time I am traveling with two people—an American woman, a Balinese man—who spend half a year in California and the other half here. They work together as a husband-wife team designing trips of a very special kind. I think of them now as guides through both the outer and the inner worlds. They know the airfares, the home-stays, the good and not-so-good restaurants, where to shop, the back roads and the beaches. They also know the legends, the lore of herbs, village psychics and trance-dancers, the fears and devotions that shape daily living.

Judy Slattum studied costume and stage design in Dallas and at the University of Oklahoma. On her first trip to Bali, back in 1978, she came to look at masks—a three-month visit that changed her life. Behind the masks she found the elaborate dance/drama and rich mythology, and behind that a mysterious island world where the artistic and the sacred have always inter-mingled. She has come back twenty-five times, as researcher, writer, lecturer, tour leader, now the blonde daughter-in-law, the blue-eyed wife of a Balinese eldest son.

I have never traveled with a mask expert. On Bali it can be a real advantage. Her head is filled with stories like this one.

"There is a little island off the southern coast called Nusa Penida," she said yesterday, explaining how a certain bearded and leonine *Barong* had come to look so outrageously fierce. "Long ago there was a demon-king who from time to time would cross to Bali and pillage the towns. He was said to be afraid of only one thing: himself. So the Balinese in that region created a mask that was a mirror-image of the demon-king. The next time he came up the beach, they held it high. And it worked! When he saw himself approaching, he turned and fled and never returned. That is why this otherwise demonic and frightful mask is looked upon as a protective spirit."

Her partner, I Madé Surya, grew up in the capitol city of Denpasar, son of a priest. An economist by training, a mountain climber, a dancer, a linguist, he is also a devout Hindu, as are most Balinese. This is my first time traveling with a Hindu. Here is the kind of thing that can happen.

Driving up from the airport we were passing through an inland town, and he stopped their four-wheel-drive Toyota next to a street stand where he bought some small offerings for a temple he knew he'd be visiting later on. These were little plaited baskets which held a few flowers, bits of rice, and holy water. He laid two in the back seat. The third he shoved into the glove box. He lit an incense stick, waved some of the smoke into the box, shut the lid, and switched on the ignition. He would never have mentioned this, but I was curious.

"Do you always keep an offering in the glove box?"

"Yes," said Surya.

He was driving again, eyes on the busy, mid-town road.

"To bless the car?" I asked. "To insure a safe trip?"

"Yes. And I guess to remind myself of what I am doing."

"What about the incense? Why did you wave that smoke in there?"

"The incense is the witness."

"Of what?"

"To witness that the proper feeling accompanies the offering."

I was impressed. I tend to take cars very seriously. As a native Californian, I knew in my bones that driving itself is an act of faith. But I had never before met anyone who routinely and on a daily basis blessed his vehicle and its welfare on the road.

LOCAL
MUSIC

After one night at Devi Sri, I move to Oka Wati's Sunset Bungalows, in the up-country village of Ubud, where Judy and Surya have their headquarters. Oka Wati herself comes from a long-time Ubud family. Her food is excellent, the mattresses are firm, the water runs both hot and cold. Each morning breakfast appears outside my door, fresh papaya, banana pancake, a pot of industrial-strength coffee. Maybe the coffee gives me visions, but by my second day here, after the jet lag subsides, I come to see this little bungalow as more than a cozy place to lay my head.

At Oka Wati's you do not get a telephone. You do not get AT&T or Sprint or Vibra-bed or the little canisters of hair conditioner above the sink, no TV in the room, no Home Box Office or VCR or CNN for Headline News. But maybe you get another kind of Discovery Channel. You get roosters crowing from the farms nearby and from the cages of the shops along Monkey Forest Road. You get green rice fields that make a wet sizzle when it rains, and the occasional shout from the old man who patrols the fields and scares the birds away. After a rain you get frogs celebrating new water in the paddies. "The original Balinese music," Surya says.

On the floor of my room the tiles make a mandala pattern. On the carved doors and doorway, mythic figures are depicted. Over a low wall outside the window I can see a family temple. In a cleared space, open to the air, there are half a dozen shrines topped with pyramids of thatch—a shrine to the ancestors, a shrine to Brahma, Vishnu, and Shiva. Gunung Agung, Bali's sacred mountain, has a shrine here too, a place of its own among the deities.

Each day a young woman brings fresh offerings, tiny baskets of flowers and rice. She will leave one at each shrine, murmur a prayer, wave her hand. Two or three times a day an offering basket will appear at the corner of my porch, on the porches of all the bungalows. Like Surya's car, each room is blessed, and the stairs we walk upon.

As soon as you check into a place like Oka Wati's you enter a loaded realm, on this island layered with patterns of gesture and ritual, symbols and ceremony. Long before you can begin to know what all the imagery is about and how deep the layers go, it is working on you, just as the eyes of the Balinese begin to work on you. Whether you know it or not, you are being blessed, literally, two or three times a day, simply by being here.

LEGENDS

Feeling blessed does not mean you have finally been admitted into Paradise—though that word continues to appear in the ads and in the guidebooks. I wish they'd stop talking about paradise. It just gets your hopes up. It leads to articles like one I read on the plane, about a paradise that has somehow been "lost."

Usually the writer is referring to an island. Sometimes Bali. Sometimes Hawai'i. Sometimes the Seychelles, in the Indian Ocean. Sometimes it is California, which was originally thought to be an island "on the right hand of the Indies . . . very close to the side of the Terrestrial Paradise . . . and in the whole island there was nothing but gold."6 This is how California was first described, in a Spanish romance called *The Adventures of Esplandian*, a fantastical novel of the sixteenth century, and it is an idea that has lingered in the imagination ever since, despite four centuries of news to the contrary.

In these articles the location will change, from writer to writer, from magazine to magazine, but it is always a place with a seductive legend attached, a legend of the blissful life. Certain questions are asked, time and time again, usually in a headline.

"Is There Trouble in Paradise?"

"Are There Weeds in the Garden?"

"Are Things Not What They Used To Be?"

And there is a recurring tone: disappointment. Sometimes a sense of betrayal. As if one of life's basic promises has been broken. The writer then begins to take apart this legendary location, listing the many ways it has fallen from grace.

My heart goes out to these writers. Paradise has never existed anywhere except in the mind. But in the mind it lives on and on. Over the years various earthly places have been chosen as examples, places that flesh out our hopes and dreams, if only we can get there. We are all conspirators in this. We all carry around old yearnings for that idyllic spot we can someday reach or return to.

"So in the soul of man," wrote Melville in *Moby Dick* a hundred and forty years ago, "there lies one insular Tahiti, full of peace and joy, but encompassed by all the horrors of the half-known life. God keep thee! Push not off from that isle, thou canst never return."

When you actually arrive at one of these spots, you may be able to prolong the dream for a while—even now, in the latter days of the twentieth century—by remaining outside the patterns of daily life, under the beach umbrella, or close to the destination resort. Paradise is really an outsider's expectation, a vision that is keyed to keeping your distance from the local realities. Hawai'i may have been a paradise for some of the earliest visitors, who came ashore for a while, then sailed away again. It has never been paradise for the Hawaiians, who have always had their daily lives to live.

The same is true here in Bali, where the weather is balmy and the earth is abundant. No one is starving, and there are no homeless, because everyone has a family somewhere and a family compound to return to. It is an island of musicians and dancers and painters and carvers. And the Balinese laugh a lot. They like to laugh. But there are also demons in the air, trials and temptations, and evil forces they must constantly guard against, spirits that can make you sick. Moisture and insects eat away at the buildings. And the rice farmers work long hours pushing water buffalo through the mud for their three or four hundred dollars per year.

Yesterday I was wandering through the labyrinthine marketplace at Kuta Beach, where low stalls seem to run for miles along the beach road. Following a swept dirt path between the rows of hanging shirts and trousers, I stopped to look at some bracelets. The stall was filled with rings of shell and silver and painted wood. The young man who approached from out of the dark cave at the rear of the stall looked about twenty, slender and smoothly brown, with hooded eyes. He wore jeans and a white shirt unbuttoned. You could see that a large tattoo covered most of his chest.

After I had touched a few bracelets and inquired about prices, I mentioned the tattoo. He opened his shirt to display the image. Over his thinly muscular breastbone there was a skull, with large feathered wings on either side and, pointing into the top of the skull, a hypodermic needle.

"What is it?" I asked.

"*Garuda*," he said, referring to the feathered birdman who flies through brilliant skies and evidently flies through darkness too.

"What about the needle?"

"You don't know what it is?" he asked with a grin.

"You tell me."

As if aiming at his forearm he pushed a thumb against two fingers, looking at me significantly.

"The needle that makes your face a skull," I said, "and makes your head grow wings."

"Yes," he said, with a wide and hungry grin. "You understand."

The look on his face was as familiar, in its way, as the look I saw today on the face of another young man, a taxi driver, who reminds me of a lot of young husbands back in the states. His name is Nyoman. He is twenty-five. He does some driving for Judy and Surya, airport runs and so forth. Nyoman and his wife both work to make ends meet. They have a son age three-and-a-half. They live in the family's compound. Relatives watch the child, the wife cooks in a local restaurant every afternoon, while he spends his days piloting visitors around the island. The growth of tourism has been good for business, but it hasn't made his life much easier.

"More visitor, more bungalow," he says. "More traffic. More motor bike. More noise."

"And more money for you?"

"Yes. Sure. But all cost more too."

"How about food?"

"Everything. Food more. Clothes more. Gasoline more."

I ask him if he owns his van, and he shakes his head. He leases it. "Too expensive to buy. And you? In America, you have a car?"

"Yes."

"Mercedes Benz?"

"A Japanese car. A Mazda."

"Good. This is Japanese. A Mitsubishi."

"How much do you pay for gasoline?"

"Five hundred rupiah, one liter."

"That's cheaper than in the US right now."

"A lot for Bali though."

On his tape deck he plays Bob Marley and the Wailers. His T-shirt says "Cadillac Man." He is dark and husky, with a thick black mustache, a ready smile that squeezes up around his eyes. He has been awake all night sitting with family members in another compound, grieving over a death. "We sit with them and tell stories and keep them company so they will not feel bad."

For him it is both a duty and a pleasure. Family comes first, he says. Family, community, tradition. "We are like fish in the sea," he says. "If we travel somewhere, another town, or Java, we rent five rooms, but we all sleep in two rooms. We like to be . . ." He rolls his hands, one over the other. "We all swim together."

IN CONRAD
COUNTRY

All day the clouds hover, yesterday and today, the air gets thicker, and the clothes get thick against the skin. At 6 PM the rain comes at last, without wind, a softly falling, steady rain that makes a hissing in the rice fields. Water drips off the raggedy edges of my bungalow's roof, as the rain falls and then as the night falls around the rain, and suddenly there is nothing to do, nowhere to be and no way to get there.

When you are this close to the equator, the nights are always long. If you have a lightbulb it is small and dim. Up-country, when the world shuts down and the dirt roads turn to mud, you can understand what Joseph Conrad was getting at in *Lord Jim*, as Marlowe sits on a verandah somewhere not too far from here, while the red ends of his listeners' cigars punctuate the darkness. It takes Marlowe all night to tell aloud the three-hundred-and-fifty-page story that is the novel.

Certain commentators have complained about this. Not persuasive, they have said. A belabored literary device. In his Author's Note to the 1917 edition, Conrad mentions reviewers who had "argued that no man could have been expected to talk all that time, and other men to listen so long. It was not, they said, very credible."

My guess is that such objections have been raised by readers who had not spent a night in the equatorial tropics, where time stretches and stretches and stretches, and dark comes early every season of the year.

THE MAN WHO PREFERS TO BE ROBBED IN JAKARTA

In Denpasar I meet a screenwriter, a fellow from Jakarta who happens to be spending a couple of weeks here. We are introduced at an outdoor restaurant, and we talk for quite a while because his English is very good, and he is eager to reminisce about Los Angeles, where he lived for a couple of years.

"For those of us on Java," he says with a laugh, "Bali is a bit like Catalina Island for Southern California. A very pleasant vacation spot and not too far from shore."

He calls himself Willi. He is dark and lean, and a Moslem, as are most Javanese, though not the kind of Moslem we most often hear about, the desert-formed Moslems, the Arabs, the Iraqis, the nomads and the Berbers of North Africa. Willi is a man of the tropics, an equatorial Moslem who has spent most of his life a long way from Mecca, thousands of miles south and west, in a humid land where mangoes grow.

Buddhism and Hinduism flourished on Java for many centuries before Islam came along. Before Buddhism there were animal gods and volcano deities you still hear mentioned from time to time. Each of these ways of seeing and believing has left its imprint and added its flavor to what is in the air of Indonesia and in the statuary around the temples. Somehow this whole history shows in Willi's face, sounds in his voice. He also speaks Japanese, in addition to Javanese (his native tongue) and Bahasa Indonesia (the national language). He claims to be a Moslem. His sense of humor is Indian. He is a fatalist, but a jolly fatalist. When he talks about fate or the various forms of human folly, he laughs merrily. His black, luminous eyes are always filled with mirth.

We sip long-neck bottles of Bintang Beru and sample foods coming toward us from the restaurant's kitchen—froglegs, barbecued shrimp, the vegetable dish called *gado-gado,* the little spicy kebab sticks they call *satay*—and we talk about Los Angeles.

I have seen just enough of his home city to have the impression that Jakarta and L.A. are alike in at least a few ways. There is a reliance on oil trading and the wealth this has generated. There is the ethnic mixing—in this case, the Javanese and Malay and Chinese, with the centuries of Dutch Colonial rule still lingering (they called it "Batavia"). There are vast districts filled with millions of people and wide boulevards thick with traffic day and night.

I tell him I remember secretly giving thanks that I did not have to drive in such traffic, that I could hail a cab and sit back and shut my eyes and not watch what appeared to be the utter chaos of buses, scooters, vans, cars, bikes, and motorcycles with protruding sidecars.

Willi's face lights up with shocked delight. "No rules of the road in Java?" he says with a laugh. "Quite the contrary. There are four. If you master them, you will have no trouble at all."

"And what would those be?"

"Pick. Big. Flow. No See, No Face."

He takes them one at a time, his shoulders happily shaking.

Flow, he tells me, has two dimensions—speed and shape. In general, speed will increase or decrease depending on the number of buses, pedicabs, and speedbumps to be contended with. So you ride the flow of the speed. Meanwhile, remember that the concept of lanes is very fluid. As traffic lanes form and dissolve, re-form and disappear, you always go with the flow.

Pick. A vehicle with so much as an inch of advantage on another has the right to turn first, to pass, to move. Whether this advantaged vehicle is coming from the right or left makes no difference. And in these decisions, courtesy is never a factor.

Big. No matter what else is happening, the larger the vehicle, the more influence it has.

No See, No Face. Keep your eyes straight ahead. Don't look into the faces of other drivers or glance toward nearby vehicles. As long as you have not acknowledged another vehicle, you can make any move that comes to mind. If two cars happen to be approaching on a two-lane road, one preparing to turn left and the other preparing to pass a third car, the game is to follow your chosen route and never make eye contact. Once you have so much as glanced at the other driver, you bring upon yourself more responsibility.

I tell Willi he must have survived pretty well in California.

"On the freeways, yes, I did very well indeed. I was fully prepared. But on the streets . . ." His brown face opens with a melancholy smile. "Not so good."

I ask him what happened, and he tells me his California story.

He was there as a reporter, writing feature pieces for a Tokyo paper. "I was also there to guard my wife, who was taking courses at USC. Here is the kind of thing I would be faced with. I had been to Universal Studios for the tour, since I was already starting to be interested in film. Afterward I was crossing the street toward a bus stop. I had a mustache at the time, with a beard on my chin, and a coat that was perhaps looking a bit worn and thin at the lapels. Well, a woman who was standing there waiting for the same bus saw me coming and she cried out, 'Don't you take one more step toward me or I will call the police!'

"She had seen my features, you see, and perhaps thought I was Vietnamese. There were many Southeast Asians in Los Angeles in those days. She just assumed I was on my way to rob her, or that I was somehow a danger to her. Her cries made everyone else turn and look at me as if I were a criminal, just for walking toward the bus stop, and this filled me with enormous sadness. In her eyes I was a threat. It gave me more sadness than being robbed, though that too was a very sad day. Or rather, a sad night, since this time I was coming back to our apartment. I had just put my hand on the gate when a car stopped at the curb, and three men climbed out, calling to me.

"It was a fine-looking car, I might add, so I had no thought that they wanted to rob me. Here in Indonesia no person with a car such as that would stop another on the street to rob him of his money. One man had on a sporting outfit, as if he had been playing tennis. White shorts. An expensive knit shirt. White shoes. When he pointed the weapon at me I thought at first it was the end of a tennis racket. I thought this was some sort of joke. I said, 'What do you want? This twenty-five cent piece?'

"I thought I was playing along with the joke. I happened to have a quarter in my shirt pocket and I showed it to the fellow with the weapon, which turned out to be a double-barreled shotgun. He hit me here, across my face, with the end of the gun, then he shoved the barrel into my chest and said, 'Give me your wallet, man!' I knew then that this was no joke. I gave him my wallet. They drove away. I could not understand it. They were much richer than I was at the time, judging by their clothing and by the car. I had no car. I had no tennis outfit. After that experience, alas, I could not enjoy my stay. I was always on guard, wondering what would happen to me next."

By the end of his tale I am feeling guilty for the mean streets of my homeland, wishing things had gone better for this gentle-hearted and harmless man. I tell him I'm sorry he had such a difficult time.

His hand touches my arm. "Forgive me. I did not tell you these stories in order to extract an apology."

"It must have been a relief to come back to Jakarta."

He is laughing again, his eyes liquid, luminous, filled with amazement now.

"I have been robbed many times, you know, and not only in Los Angeles. I was robbed in Honolulu, and more than once in Jakarta I have been robbed, though it is not the same. All these cities are dangerous, I suppose. But not in the same way. Thieves are not the same. In Java they use knives, not shotguns. Guns are against the law. The common citizen cannot own one. I once told a thief, as I handed him my money, 'These few thousand rupiah are all I have remaining in the world.' And you know what he did? The man handed it back to me. He was a thief by necessity, but he was still a man of honor. He was stealing to eat, or perhaps to feed his family, out of desperation, but not to buy drugs. I was touched by this. I had already lost the money, you see, surrendered it to him. To get it back was such an unexpected blessing, I felt compelled to reward the poor fellow. I gave him half the money. I split it with him."

A dessert has been set before us, rice jellies in coconut milk, and some strong coffee. We sip the coffee, try the dessert.

"Sometimes I ask myself why I have been robbed so often. And I remember that mine was a difficult birth. It was—what is the term?—a breach birth? All these robberies. Maybe I was not supposed to be born."

I hear no self-pity. The idea seems to amuse him and satisfy him. It occurs to me that he has not mentioned calling the police or looking for ways to punish any of his thieves. Somehow he sees himself as both victim and accomplice, as if since long before birth his fate has been hurtling toward him down a two-lane road. Had he kept his eyes averted, according to the fourth rule of the road on Java, things might have worked out differently. But he is the kind of fellow who makes eye contact, and with that has come this curious burden of responsibility for whatever befalls him. As we sip our coffee his eyes gaze into mine, merry, ancient, boyish, dark and innocent, the vulnerable sage.

THE DAY FOR
BLESSING
METAL OBJECTS

On the Balinese calendar one day is set aside for blessing all objects that contain metal. Family by family, everyone takes part. As the eldest són, Surya has many duties, many ceremonies where his presence is expected, and this is one of them.

From the rice fields and villages around Ubud, we drive south into Denpasar, which is full of vehicles and smoky haze, shocking you, like any city does, when entered from the back roads—cars, motorbikes, traffic snarl, gasoline pumps, parades of kids in school uniforms, rows of cluttered shops. From one of the busiest boulevards we take a turn onto a quieter street, then swing into an alley, and we arrive at the compound his family has occupied for seven generations.

His father is here, his sister, and his great-aunt, now widowed and in her seventies. She is the preparer of family offerings, a daily task which she attends to on an open-air porch set aside for this one activity. Today has been especially busy. The women have been at it since early morning, plaiting fronds, boiling rice, cutting up banana leaves. Near the table where they work, a long wooden box has been filled with implements gathered from the cooking shed, from the garden, from the building where the antiques and ceremonial gear are stored—chisels, saws, hammers, knives, spoons, an elderly kris, a sword Surya recently brought back from Borneo, an old blowpipe that has been in their family for a century, wooden, maybe ten feet long, with a metal point at one end, so that it doubles as a spear.

Surya is trim and vigorous, with a directness of gaze, a worldly air that comes from traveling widely, along with a perpetual sense of wonder and delight. He takes a great, boyish pleasure in lifting this blowpipe, as he holds one end to the light to show me the straight barrel drilled through a single cylinder of iron-tough wood. He holds it to his mouth and shows me how to propel the dart with a strong pop of the breath at one end. I ask him if anyone in his family has ever used it. "Yes," he says. "My grandfather. Against the Dutch."

Before the blessings begin, the household visitors have to be welcomed and purified. That means me and Judy. Like the others, we have already donned our sarongs and sashes, the respectful dress for a Balinese Hindu ceremony or temple visit. The fact is, this event falls somewhere in between, since these blessings all take place within view of the family temple.

In a cleared and open space next to the low wall around the compound, the thatch-topped shrines stand in a row. One is for the ancestors, where the ashes of seven generations have been buried. A smaller version is for the guardian of the ancestors' shrine. There is a shrine to Taksu, the deity who presides over each person's talent or gift in life, and a shrine dedicated to the earth ("the Earth Mother," Surya points out), and a shrine to Gunung Agung, the dormant volcano that rises some thirty miles to the north and west. From the road into the city we had seen it. From the presence of these shrines, in every household temple on the island, you begin to grasp the mountain's role, the power that is acknowledged every day and somehow recognized—like the ancestors are recognized—in every ceremony, in all these daily and seasonal observances.

Now Surya has a cup of holy water previously blessed by a high priest in the neighborhood. Using a blossom as a wand, he sprinkles this over our heads and upon our outstretched hands. The same water is then sprinkled upon the heap of metal implements, where offerings have been laid—all of which is a prologue to the larger matter of blessing the two vehicles Surya and

Judy have driven down from Ubud for the occasion, their aging VW and their four-wheel-drive jeep-style Toyota.

They are parked side by side in the dirt-floored carport that looks out upon the yard of shrines. Here two tables have been set up, where offerings have been arranged on raised ceramic platters—small plaited baskets, incense sticks, rice, and rice cakes, many flowers, boiled eggs, half a fried chicken. Circles and tassels made of young, yellow-green leaves hang from the bumpers, and over the grilles.

Using a flower, Surya's diminutive mother sprinkles holy water on the cars, praying softly with her eyes closed. She scatters rice across the hoods and prays again. From a bottle she sprinkles more water, spilling it onto the ground between the cars, with a prayer each time, and more rice strewn, and more sprinkling, from a bottle of *brem* (rice wine) and from a bottle of *arak* (rice brandy). Finally small frond baskets holding flowers and bits of rice are set under each right front wheel, so the cars will roll over them. This will complete the blessing, Surya tells me. Protective energy from the offering will rise up into the cars and also guard against bad luck in case something unexpectedly gets hit, an animal perhaps.

Later, as we start back toward Ubud, the city boulevards and the roads outside the city have a festive and holiday look. All the cars have been decorated. We see buses with plaited tassels hanging from the side mirrors, tourist vans with little circles of woven leaves held down by the windshield wipers or suspended from a headlight. By late afternoon of the Day for Blessing Metal Objects, knives and spoons and chisels and hammers and cars and jeeps and vans all over Bali have been attended to, spoken to, purified and cleansed.

MASKS
AND
DANCERS

Every day or so Judy and Surya head out to another town or village, to witness a wedding or a cremation, or to visit the house compound of a healer or a working artist like Ketut Kantor. He lives in Batuan, about ten miles south of Ubud. His specialty is the mask dance called *topeng*.

Driving through the palm-lined countryside, we pass women young and old bearing baskets on their heads. Past the center of the village we turn off the rutted main road onto a narrow dirt track lined with weather-eaten, mold-crumbled walls of concrete and brick. Along his entryway five motorbikes are parked.

As Kantor welcomes us I feel I have been blessed again, in yet another way, by being given this glimpse inside the low stone wall that contains his sleeping porches, his garden, his cooking shed. He is not a fellow traveler from America would ordinarily meet, since he speaks little English and performs mostly for other Balinese. But he is one of the many allies Judy and Surya have cultivated over the years.

Inside the compound of Kantor the dancer, everything is going on at once. Dogs and chickens run loose. Roosters are crowing. Under one thatch roof a young woman stirs a steaming metal pot of stew. Under another, women sit on low, mat-covered tables as they prepare offerings for a wedding a few days hence. There is a narrow rice house lifted off the ground and steeply roofed with galvanized metal to discourage mice. Next to it stands a shrine wrapped with black-and-white-checkered cloth. Coconuts are piled near the shrine, gathered from the surrounding palms, and a heap of rusty red bananas.

Two men in sarongs and thong slippers are laying some cement. Scampering past them comes Ketut's two-year-old grandson wearing a pair of "Batman" shorts. One of the men is singing a plaintive song, and the little boy stops to dance, just for fun, a kid playing around, maybe showing off for the visitors. Kitut Kantor learned topeng from his father, who learned from his father. Now in the grandson you can already see the moves forming. At two he has the shoulder lift, the supple wrist, the chubby fingers bent back and extended.

After a couple of minutes he loses interest and squats to hitch up his shorts. The workmen laugh. Everyone laughs. Then we join Ketut under the peaked thatch roof of a small pavilion, where drums hang from a post, along with a picture of his father.

We are here to watch him dress for a performance. According to Judy and Surya, dance/drama is a key for understanding Bali—along with the idea that they have no word here for *art* or *artist*. To be human is to be creative. To begin to know the masks and the dances, you meet the dancer where he lives his life.

Kitut is about fifty, a short and husky fellow with a soft voice and gentle eyes. His teeth are stained brown from betel-nut. His sturdy features make me think of Anthony Quinn. With late sun slanting in past palms and nearby porches, we watch him lace up beaded leggings of brown velvet. A young assistant helps him strap a ritual sword across his shoulders, wraps him in a white sarong. He dons a cape of stenciled gold that resembles brocade, with beaded epaulets in three layers, and over these a three-layered collar. He is grinning and sweating at the finish, strapped and wrapped in the equatorial heat, and ready to lead us up the road to the neighborhood temple.

There are over two hundred thousand temples on this island ninety miles wide and forty across (half the size of Los Angeles County). They range from the small family temples seen inside every compound, to those that serve the whole society, like Besakih, the Mother Temple, a small city of courtyards and pyramid towers on the southern slope of Gunung Agung, where the sacred mountain is a looming wall beyond the towers and the air is as vibrant and thick as the air at Kilauea. Meanwhile, in each village there are three local temples: *Pura Puseh,* the temple of origins; *Pura Desa,* the temple for ceremonies involving the living; and *Pura Dalem,* the temple of the dead. This afternoon we trooped down a dusty back road to the Pura Desa, where a gamelan orchestra is already out front and warming up.

Through a gateway we can see Kitut in the courtyard. His masks are in there too, in a long box in front of an altar. Performers do all sorts of things to center themselves before going onstage. In Bali a performer like Kitut goes into the temple to bless his masks, pray for guidance, ask ancestors for support. During an interview with Judy he once said that the first time he performed publicly, away from his village, his father arranged for a special ceremony "where I was purified by a Bramin priest. As part of this ceremony I was 'married to the masks' I would be using."

He makes his entrance through the high, narrow gate, the two halves of a split pyramid. He wears a gold headdress and a brown mask with bright red lips, its eyes bulging with the white bug eyes of the Prime Minister. As he enters, the temple becomes a set, and its foreyard a stage. His body is tight and electrifying, the knees jutting. As he hops down the stairs, the gongs and drums accent each motion, the tiny jerks of his head, the undulating fingers, the quivering thumbs.

He does not speak. This is solo pantomime, the mask and the costume brilliant, exaggerated. There is a high sense of theatre, though he is not acting a scene. In some other way he casts a spell. Part of it is in the music, hypnotic and relentless. Part of it is location. Being outside a temple makes this more than entertainment. It is like the early days of European drama, when the priest/actors re-lived New Testament scenes on the cathedral steps or at the altar.

He prances and he preens and holds the crowd captive, hops away at the end of each dance, through the gate and into the courtyard, and comes back again, each time wearing another mask. The Village Chief. The Pig-Headed King. The Underdog. The Trickster.

BELIEVERS

Oka Wati's garden, early morning.

A low stage looks out upon the breezeless profusion of bougainvillea, plumeria, hibiscus both yellow and red, ferns, and banana palms. The dozen travelers who spent yesterday in Batuan with Kitut Kantor now listen to Judy and Surya talk about topeng and how it works. Standing on the stage they make an impressive team. She is blonde, vivacious, with a sudden smile and a costumer's flair for dramatic clothes. He is swarthy and athletic, with an alert face sharpened by the black mustache, the trimmed chin beard.

"The dancer," Judy says, "is not acting out a day in the life of the Prime Minister. It is not a *scene* to express a certain emotion, like fear or danger. The idea is to project a source of energy. It will differ from character to character, which is the great challenge for the dancer. For each character he must reveal that kernel of radiant energy that is true to this character's essence."

She pulls her fists in close to her belt, for emphasis. Her eyes are shining. She has a radiance of her own, which seems kindled by this world she has returned to time and time again.

For a moment Surya gazes down at the tiles of the stage. He is barefoot, wearing T-shirt and jeans. Then he springs forward with his knees bent, his toes upraised, his thumbs aquiver as if they have lives apart. He has studied traditional dance since childhood—*baris* (warrior) and *kecak* (monkey dance) as a young man, topeng for the past several years. In seconds he is able to charge the air, just as Judy described it. He wears no mask, so you can see at close range the steady black eyes that look toward you and through you in fierce concentration.

His body relaxes. He smiles a broad, pleased, friendly smile. He likes doing this. He likes sharing what he knows about his island. He picks up a mask and holds it at arm's length, regarding its lacquered stare. His nasal voice is rich, resonant. "You don't just put on a mask. You first must look at it, absorb it, and after you are inside it, you must remember all its characteristics."

As he slips it over his face, Judy begins to talk about various moves that create the surprise and suspense of Balinese theatre. Each move is acted out by Surya.

The dancer will plant his feet, she says, but lift the toes, which deliberately throws off the center of gravity and adds high tension to the body. The dancer will follow the Laws of Opposition.

"If you want to go left, you begin by going right. If you want to go up, you must first go down, drop the shoulders, bend the knees. So the dancer never moves in a straight line. It is actually the reverse, an abundance of movement that holds us spellbound."

Her voice is animated. His moves are supple and quick. As I watch and listen, I am thinking, How many people can give you this double perspective—the passion of the discoverer, and the knowledge that is in the blood? They see both ways across the Pacific, and they have the charm of believers. In our age of cynicism and disbelief, they want you to believe that the deeply rooted spirit of this ancient place has so far survived the well-known hazards of western intervention and modern times.

IN THE MARIANAS

IV

SAIPAN
AND
TINIAN

Over the Arafura Sea, the China Sea,
　Coral Sea, Pacific
chains of volcanoes in the dark
　　— Gary Snyder, *The Back Country* (1968)

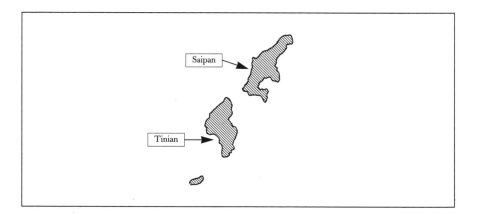

The Marianas: the Philippine Sea is to the west and the Pacific Ocean to the east.
Japan is north-northwest, Papua New Guinea to the south.

BATTLE
LINES

Each of these islands is a world unto itself, with its own history, its own mystique, and its own lesson to impart, depending upon what you're ready for on the day you step off the boat or the plane. On Kyushu I found a mirror, on the Big Island a temple of igneous rock. Bali was another kind of temple. And Saipan was a memorial to the paradox of war.

The flight back from Bali had a layover on Guam. I took the opportunity to linger in the Marianas and make a side trip to visit our daughter, who happened to be working out there, at a beach hotel. I could not have known, from afar and in advance, how loaded is the atmosphere around Saipan. Like a cloud you can't quite see, like a translucent mist that never dissolves, the legacy of the Pacific war floats and hovers, as it still hovers around all the shores and islands where the legendary campaigns were waged. In the memories of island families the stories live on, to be told and retold. In the waters offshore, old relics lie submerged.

I was taken back to my boyhood days and the early fears that San Francisco would soon be invaded by sea and by air, and that the West Coast itself could become a battleground. After Pearl Harbor was attacked, and for several months into 1942, my folks were prepared at any moment to see fleets of bombers appearing on the horizon. All over the city the western-facing sides of the streetlights were painted black, and our bags stayed packed, for the fast escape to somewhere farther inland.

In my bedroom I built models of the Mitsubishi bombers and pitted them against our twin-tailed P-38s. Each Saturday, all through the '40s, in the Irving Theater there in the city's Sunset District, before the double feature, I watched the battle coverage in Time Marches On. *I watched Lloyd Nolan and John Wayne reenact the fall of Corregidor, our tiny fortress in the middle of Manila Bay, and the costly landings at Guadalcanal and Tarawa. As the war unfolded, I listened to the stories of uncles and cousins from Huntsville and Baton Rouge and Fort Worth who would pass through the city, to spend a night or two with us before climbing aboard the troopships.*

One of them, my dad's older brother, flew as a navigator for the Army Air Corps. He too grew up in Texas, where he did his training. On his way to the South Pacific he let me wear his flight jacket. When he came through town the second time, heading home at war's end, he told us of all the places he'd been, which planes he'd flown in, and which islands he had seen from the cockpit. Then he gave me the jacket. It was the real thing, the color of mahogany, with a fur collar, shoulder patches, his name and rank above the pocket. Inside that jacket I was somehow transported, flying fantasy missions side by side with my uncle.

In later years I saw a thousand photographs, read The Naked and the Dead *and* From Here to Eternity. *I talked with veterans of numerous campaigns, and spent my own time in the military.*

None of this prepares you for the actual scene of the battle, which is what always brings it home. That hits you in the heart and in the belly. Seeing Saipan was like visiting Pearl Harbor for the first time and seeing the sunken turrets of the U.S.S. Arizona *and knowing that the flames from that ghastly holocaust still heat the air above the bay.*

Saipan is even more profound, in my view, and more telling now, though it will never have Pearl Harbor's high profile. From Hawai'i it's four thousand miles farther west, and an hour north of Guam by inter-island shuttle. Americans seldom stop there, except on official business, or in search of exotic diving. I wouldn't have stopped there myself, had it not been for what you might call this family connection.

AN ISLAND
WITHIN
AN ISLAND

🌿 Our daughter has been hired by a big resort, along with a dozen other recent graduates from West Coast campuses, who bring their exuberance, their youthful energy, their willingness to make a short-term commitment in exchange for a season in the Tropics. She is out here for a year or so, with a room and three good meals a day, a salary, and a round-trip ticket. As a member of an employee's family, I too have a free room, courtesy of the hotel. If I can get myself to Saipan, I have a meal pass waiting for me and access to all facilities. Not that I am here to slide down the water slide and splash into the simulated grotto that curves around next to the poolside bar. But I could if I wanted to. It comes with the pass.

The Northern Marianas is a US Commonwealth, and this hotel, the Pacific Island Club, is American owned. I happen to be the only American guest. Almost all the paying customers are young, upscale families and newlyweds who fly down from Tokyo and Kobe and Nagoya for three or four days or a week. It is their offshore island, three hours south, their Bermuda, their Azores, and this resort is like the destination resorts you come across everywhere these days, sufficiently self-contained and sealed off from whatever lies beyond its perimeter, you never have to leave the grounds. It is an island within an island, its own closed system, providing for all your needs.

Our daughter, Gabrielle, knows this. Maybe it is starting to get to her, the sense of unreality. "We're in a time warp, Dad. There are no seasons here.

The temperature never changes. Every day is the same. Every night is Friday night. Every morning is Sunday morning. There are always loads of people around. It's a perpetual weekend. And me? I never have to go shopping. Even the toilet paper is taken care of. The food is there. The room is there. Weeks go by, and you never have to leave the place."

I'm not worried about her. She is learning things. She is learning about real and unreal. She started out as a recreation leader. She has been promoted to supervisor. She has learned to handle a four-wheel drive vehicle, because from time to time her job will take her across the island, past the paved roads, which end outside Susupe, the main town. In order to accommodate the guests, she is also learning Japanese at a local community college. At breakfast in the hotel's vast dining room we sit at a table with three young women from Osaka, and I watch her engage them in polite conversation.

"*Ohayo gozai-masu . . . Haji-me-mashite . . .*" ("Good morning. It's nice to meet you. Where are you from? How do you like the food?")

I'm impressed. I'm the pleased father watching her try out new skills. In this moment she reminds me of Jeanne, whose spoken Japanese is tinged not so much with an American accent, as with American body moves. Even among strangers Gabby's smile is expansive. Her manner is forthright, her gaze direct. At the same time, with the very speaking of these words, something else begins to show, something latent. Like Jeanne, she has an inner ear for the music of this language, though in all her years growing up in California she never spoke it. Out here on the farther side of the Pacific, something Asian comes rising into her voice. I think how pleased Jeanne would be to hear this, to see this, pleased on behalf of her father, who didn't make it back to Japan yet always hoped his children and his grandchildren would somehow be in touch with the culture of his birthplace.

But this trip is only partly about our daughter. Though she is the reason I have flown to Saipan, I see that the island itself is what I have to write about, and the apparitions lurking here. They add a second layer of unreality to the place. Among the pleasure-seeking guests, invisible figures wander around, the spirits and the memories of what happened back in June 1944.

Inside the reef the water is glassy, so aquamarine, so perfectly tropical it appears to be the recreation zone of your dreams. You step out of the air-conditioned lobby into blinding sunlight. You walk past the water slide dumping guests into the pool beneath a Disneyesque pirate's ship. You pass the badminton court, and the volleyball court, and sunbathers returning from the beach, slender Japanese fellows with lime-colored glare patches under their eyes—wide receivers from outer space. You pass a little cabin where water gear is handed out, fins, face masks, thick monogrammed towels, foam rubber booties in case you have to set a foot down on the offshore coral. And from there, from the fringe of dazzlingly white sand, you can look out toward the reef where US Marines and Army amphibious units launched their first attack against this stronghold.

At the edge of the beach, right at the hotel's property line, in the shade of coco palms, there is a monument in the sand, dedicated to the US Marine Fourth Division. On the day they landed, four thousand men went down, dead or wounded. Offshore, a hundred yards away, there is a rusty and surf-eroded tank, stuck on the reef for half a century. Up the coast a mile or so, two more tanks are sitting in the water with turrets and cannons poking through the surface, old witnesses of the carnage during those two months when Saipan was granted its lurid place in history.

AFTER
THE WAR

The dining room is named for Ferdinand Magellan. He reached these islands in 1521 and claimed them for Spain. A hundred and fifty years later they were named in honor of Mariana of Austria, widow of the Spanish king, Phillip IV. Another two hundred years went by, and in 1889 Spain sold the island chain to Germany. After World War I the German Empire was divided up. Japan, being a US ally at the time, acquired the Marianas, including Saipan, and began to colonize the place. But through all these years the island was virtually unknown and unheard-of, the tiny peak of a massive underwater mountain at the edge of the deepest canyon on the planet, the Marianas Trench.

The war put it on the map. Strategically it was a key outpost in Japan's defense system, a bit like Hawai'i, vis-à-vis our west coast. Once Saipan and nearby Tinian were taken, the US military no longer had to rely on aircraft carriers to get within bombing range. We had a runway and a launch pad for the prolonged aerial attack on the Japanese mainland.

Thirty thousand troops were stationed on this tiny stretch of land, along with a resident civilian population, the colonists. The battles were fierce because the Japanese in fact were defending their home shores. On June 15, 1944, the day two US Marine divisions waded into the relentless artillery fire, the lagoon out in front of this hotel, blue-green and translucent now, turned red with blood.

From this beach, where scuba divers frolic, the US forces pushed gradually north across the island, taking ground and losing ground and retaking it, until the Japanese made their final stand at what is now labeled "the Last Command Post." The island is littered with the evidence of this campaign—old tanks, cannons, concrete bunkers where they took refuge, interior rooms and air-raid shelters hacked out of rocky cliffs. Cartridge casings still turn up on the beaches, or when a stretch of jungle land is cleared.

"Here at the hotel," Gabby tells me, "when the guys are raking the sand in the volleyball court, they will sometimes uncover old bullet shells or things will wash up in front of the guard stand, rounds of ammunition that have been out there in the lagoon for god knows how long."

We drive into the hills beyond town to see a Quonset hut that has been set aside as the storage site for such items. They accumulate until someone from the local radar station comes to haul them away for demolition. All these years after the shooting ended, the current collection—a couple of months' worth—includes some three hundred pieces of dead and live ammo, mortar shells, incendiary bombs, clips of unspent rifle cartridges encrusted with barnacles.

The most moving testimony is found in the region around the two cliffs where thousands of Japanese chose to take their own lives. The Last Command Post is a bunker built into a mountainside, with an overhanging rock face for protection. Out in front, a few hundred yards away, "Banzai Cliff" drops to the water. Here, many soldiers leaped to their deaths, or tried to. Along the edge of the cliffs you see a row of gravestones and cemetery markers, short and tall, some ornate, some simple, all with Japanese characters inscribed, erected here by family members of those who died. At the base of a single large stone there is the saying,

> It is better to light candles
> than to curse the darkness.

Nearby a small plaque says,

> Devote yourselves to the creation of
> the pacific global era—1970 AD

Directly above the Last Command Post rise the gray walls called "Suicide Cliff," eight hundred feet high, still pocked with shell holes from old artillery rounds. The top of this cliff is studded with more family shrines and markers, blocks of carved granite or marble, ceramic bowls for flowers and incense sticks. From the precipice, it is said, hundreds of civilians leaped to their deaths. They preferred this to capture by the Americans, whom they believed to be cruel and unforgiving savages. These civilians were settlers, merchants, traders, shopkeepers, hospital staff. Whole families leaped, lined up by age, with the youngest pushed off by the next oldest, until finally the father walked backward toward the edge so he would not know which would be his final step.

The campaign lasted a month. Saipan fell in July. After General Yoshige Saito conceded defeat he committed hara-kiri, kneeling toward Japan, while an aide shot him in the head. Surrender was not finalized until four months after Japan itself had surrendered to the US. There happened to be one recalcitrant army officer, Sakeo Oba, who refused to give up and who carried on a guerrilla campaign for over a year, from July 1944 until November 1945. It was quite an amazing feat. On an island four miles wide and fourteen long, and outnumbered one thousand to one, he and his troops eluded capture for sixteen months. They gave it up only after Captain Oba was shown proof that his leaders had surrendered and the war was long over.

Of the thirty thousand Japanese military personnel, almost all perished. Along with the rest of the Marianas, the island was taken over by the United States. For thirty years it was administered as part of the Trust Territory of the Pacific. English is still the official language. And yet Saipan has been virtually reoccupied. Of the eight resorts on the island, the Pacific Island Club is the only one owned by Americans, and ninety percent of its customers come from Japan. (The rest come from Australia.) The resort town brochures, the *Marianas Beach Press* and *Hafadai* (Chamorro for "hello") are all in Japanese, with no English subtitles.

It is like the irony one feels in Hawai'i, where Japanese pilots dropped the bombs that triggered the Pacific war, and where Japanese interests now control 65 percent of the hotel space. Yet it seems more ironic here, where the loss of life was far greater and where the Japanese were so utterly defeated.

TOWARD
TINIAN

Today we drive to the craggy top of Mount Topatchau, Saipan's highest peak, a conical reminder of the island chain's volcanic origins. It's not that high, 1,545 feet, but from here you can see everything, the miles of jungle, the long lagoons inside the rim of coral. We can look across toward the next island, Tinian, low and hazy green, three miles away. Gabby and her pals have been over there on diving expeditions. You can still see the runway, she says, from the days when Tinian was the departure point for the firebombing of Japan's main cities. We talk about the waves of B-29s, sometimes hundreds in a single day, that delivered one of the most systematic and devastating assaults in the history of warfare.

In the early months of 1945 half a million civilians died in urban firestorms created by bombs dropped from planes that took off from the runway on that narrow hump of land. Half a million. Can one imagine half a million deaths by firestorm? That is more than all the combat deaths suffered by United States forces during both world wars, Korea, and Vietnam. And that was a kind of prologue to the raids of early August. The Enola Gay took off from Tinian to carry the first atomic bomb twelve hundred miles north and drop it on Hiroshima.

I look at our daughter. She has actually seen that runway. She has seen the pit where they stored the nuclear devices. She has prowled around inside one of the caves where Captain Oba hid out. She has touched ammo clips carried in the landing craft back in 1944. She is beginning to grasp the meaning of World War II, where the battles had been waged, and why. For an American of her age, this is at least as rare as understanding conversational Japanese.

I too am finally beginning to understand the war I grew up with.

Is there another spot in this ocean where monuments to the sacrifices made by both nations stand so close together? Here is the marker at the edge of the blue lagoon that once turned red with the blood of thousands of Marines, and a tank still rusting on the reef, as if refusing to let them ever be forgotten. A few miles down the coast, along the edge of Banzai Cliff and Suicide Cliff, you find the ancestral altars and ceremonial stones and bowls, some of them freshly tended, with recent offerings of incense and flowers that some traveler from Nagoya or Kyoto has prayed over, perhaps wept over.

Back home in California, in Detroit, in Tennessee, people still sometimes ask one another, Who won the war? You want to ask the question here. You want to ask, Who ever wins the war? But you don't ask. What's the point, when there is no answer.

We are driving down from the top of Mount Topatchau when Gabby says matter-of-factly, "Some Japanese guys are supposed to be negotiating now to turn Tinian into a gambling island. A lot of local people are against it. But there's big money in the background. Major amounts of money. I think they'll have their way."

"I've heard about that. The Las Vegas of the Pacific."

"That's what they're saying."

"It's wild, isn't it."

"There's never been much of anything on that island," she says, "except the runway. It's eerie, when you think about casinos where all the bombers used to park."

"How do you account for these things, Gabby?"

"What things?"

"You know what I mean."

"Hey, you're the writer, dad. You tell me."

DANCING AMONG THE GHOSTS

OKINAWA, IWO JIMA, IE-JIMA

Okinawa invaded many times.
Not sink in ocean yet.
Survive Chinese.
Survive Japanese.
Survive missionaries and Americans.

— Sakini, in John Patrick's
Teahouse of the August Moon (1952)

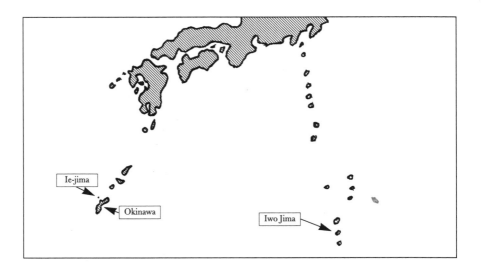

Two chains of islands run south from Japan (the southern portion of which is shown in this map). The largest island in the western chain is Okinawa; Ie-jima is a small island off Okinawa's western coast. The second southernmost island in the eastern chain is Iwo Jima; to its southeast lie the Marianas.

BORDER
LINES

The Ryukyus make a string of islands and islet clusters, a hundred and sixty or so, curving south and east from the tip of Kyushu toward Taiwan. Okinawa is the largest, in the middle of the string, a long narrow spine of an island. The name is sometimes translated to mean, "piece of rope on the horizon."

From the air it's like approaching Honolulu. An offshore reef. Turquoise lagoons, with a lime-tinted sandy bottom. A sprinkling of palms. A major airport close to shore, and a capitol city sprawling inland.

Flying in, I remembered a lecture hall in Kuala Lumpur a number of years earlier, when I was a visiting writer on a US Information Service tour, my first trip to Asia. There had already been stops in Seoul, Manila, Singapore, places I had mental pictures for ahead of time. Now I was a couple of hundred miles up the Malay peninsula and halfway to Thailand, standing at a podium in a room full of students. Most of them were Muslim, the women veiled from just below the eyes.

When it came time for questions from the crowd, a bearded fellow in a white tunic raised his hand and stood up. "In the United States," he said, "what is the general impression of Malaysia? And has that changed for you in any way since you arrived?"

As he spoke, I realized I'd had no prior impression of Malaysia, general or otherwise, and I had to tell him so. When I saw the disappointment in his face,

I tried to soften the news. "Since I had no idea what to expect here," I said, "every day has been full of illuminating surprises."

And it was true. This room filled with veils had literally stopped me in the doorway. But for him, and for me, it was another way of saying that his country, until I got there, had been as invisible as the faces of the young Muslim women whose eyes were watching, waiting.

Before I ever saw Japan, there had been a legend in my mind. Right or wrong, it was already in place, a vivid set of images gleaned from films and books and photographs and stories I'd heard. The same was true of China and Alaska and Australia and Bali and Easter Island and Tahiti and the Philippines. But Malaysia? I had to admit to myself that I had never even tried to imagine the place. As this fellow's questions continued, as he asked me about novels he'd read and popular music and presidential candidates, I realized that he knew a great deal about my country, and it filled me with shame for my ignorance of his.

Later, back home, I took a little poll among people I ran into, hoping to be reassured, I suppose, that at least I was not alone. With the exception of one seasoned and compulsive traveler, who had seen everything on earth and remembered most of it, the answers were similar. "Malaysia? Wow. I'm trying to think if I have heard of anybody who's been there."

Certain places are like that. Underreported. Infrequently visited. Not often seen on film. Somewhere beyond the borders of the American imagination. Flying in, it occurred to me that the Ryukyus have been like that. When you say the name, I asked myself, what comes to mind? What legend, if any, attaches to this little galaxy of islands between the Pacific Ocean and the China Sea?

A SEPARATE
PEOPLE

Until this trip, if I imagined the place at all, I thought distantly of the Pacific war and the roster of battle sites that moved our forces ever closer to Japan. Midway. Guadalcanal. Tarawa. Saipan. Iwo Jima. Okinawa. As I think of it now, in my personal patchwork version of this history, Iwo Jima and Okinawa have been somehow paired, linked moments in the final assault, back in the early weeks of 1945.

If anything, the battle for Iwo Jima has been the better known and more vividly recalled, perhaps because more fully covered, perhaps because of the stirring photograph that came to symbolize the American victory, one of the most widely reproduced photos of all time—five marines lifting a pole to raise the Stars and Stripes at the craggy top of Mount Suribachi.

If you were to show a group of people this famous photo now, half a century later, and say that it was taken on Okinawa, how many would protest? A veteran of that war might correct you right away. Someone else might think a moment before saying, "Hey. You sure about that?" Most would let it pass.

This is part of the ironic legacy of modern-day Okinawa, which had only one thing in common with Iwo Jima. Both islands had been transformed into fortresses. But Iwo Jima was literally a rock. Suribachi was an old crater surrounded by the ashen debris of its last eruption, out there in a cluster of rocks called the Volcano Islands, seven hundred miles due south of Tokyo, and uninhabited except for military personnel. Okinawa had a resident population of nearly half a million, and those were not colonists brought in from somewhere else. They were the colonized, politically part of Japan by that time, annexed in 1879, but ethnically and culturally distinct, a people once in possession of their separate island kingdom.

When the shooting began, these civilians were caught in the crossfire, as their homeland became the battleground for the costliest and most destructive campaign of the Pacific war. They still talk about it here. They have to talk about it. They want the rest of us to remember what they have not been able to forget. On this island that is somewhat smaller than O'ahu—sixty-five miles long, and six to eight miles wide for most of its length—there are 360 monuments to the losses suffered in April, May, and June of 1945. Every family living on the island now lost someone then.

Listening to their stories, you have to wonder about the way we use specific dates to mark when a war begins and when it ends, and then use those dates to measure time and history. The date the first shot was fired. The date the last bomb was dropped. The day the truce was signed. The world moves on to the next big countdown, the next *event.* But in the hearts of the survivors, wars don't end. In a place like Okinawa, you feel out of synch with what has gone into the annals of warfare, chronologies that depend on the finality of that final shot.

In the way that Jews have to continually tell and retell the stories of the Holocaust, and Japanese Americans retell the stories of evacuation and internment, Okinawans have to tell and retell the stories of what happened here, when one-third of their population was wiped out by the bombing and shelling and slaughter that went on for eighty-two days. The Japanese stronghold was ultimately destroyed, along with every public building, and the island's cultural showpiece, Shuri Castle, and most of the trees, and countless family tombs containing centuries of ancestral remains.

AMERICAN
STUDIES

Tourists here are mostly Japanese. They fly down from the prefectures farther north in search of somewhere warmer. Americans I've seen so far or heard about are with the military or with the consulate or have some kind of campus connection, as do Jeanne and I. We're really here to check out the island, of course, as usual. It's a rare chance to see a place so few of us get to see. But this time we also have a cover. I've been invited to speak before the American Studies Society at the University of the Ryukyus, which seemed odd to me when I first heard about it. Why would this slender island halfway between Kyushu and the Philippines have an American Studies Society and an annual conference?

Now that we've been here for a couple of days it's not so odd at all. It seems necessary. Inevitable. Their concerns run a lot deeper than an academic interest in the patterns of a foreign culture.

In the States an American Studies program is usually interdisciplinary. The idea is to bring together sources from various fields to shed some light on who we are and how our country came to be the way it is. Here the program is similar, but with one big difference. The real subject is Okinawa. To study America's habits is to study themselves and how this island came to be the way it is today.

They're in the middle of a three-year project called "The American Impact upon Okinawa since 1945." It's everything from economics, engineering, and agriculture to education, language, and literature. Here are some of the papers being presented this week:

"Private Family Housing for the US Forces in Okinawa: Historical Development and Planning"

"Cross-Cultural Contacts During the US Administration, and Changes in Clothing Habits in Okinawa"

"The Influence of the US Administration on Eating Habits in Okinawa: The Introduction and Reception of American Food Culture"

I haven't read any of the papers and won't be able to until they're translated, and I probably won't attend the lectures, since all but mine are in Japanese. But as I begin to meet and talk with people here, I see that so much more is at stake than a scholarly look at housing and clothing and food. I begin to feel the urgency you run into almost everywhere these days: the need to redefine and reclaim a cultural identity that is very much in danger of being overwhelmed.

That "impact since 1945" has included the many products and images from which there is no longer any escape. McDonald's is here. Colonel Sanders is here. Baskin & Robbins is here, along with CNN, the newest features from filmland, the shelves of video releases. Sylvester Stallone is here, and Dolly Parton, and the Global Soundtrack of favorites old and new, spilling Gershwin and Gus Kahn and Johnny Mercer and Jerome Kern and Stevie Wonder all over your seaweed soup. "But Not for Me." "Ol' Man River." "Sweet Lorraine." "Night and Day." "I Just Called to Say I Love You."

To that potent mix you have to add this last half century of our continuous military presence. Elsewhere in Japan, you have the songs and the films and the franchises in abundance, but unless you happen to live in a town like Sasebo or Yokosuka or Yokota, the average citizen seldom has to drive past an American base or deal with the comings and goings of our ships and planes, our personnel and their dependents.

In order to demolish the Japanese position here we had to demolish just about everything else. They say 94 percent of the buildings went down. The city of Naha was gone. Flattened. When the war ended, this island, along with the entire Ryukyu chain, was turned over to the United States. Our military ran it for twenty-seven years. While the villages gradually came back to life, we set about to reconstruct a sizable part of Okinawa in our own image, creating an even larger and more formidable stronghold than the one we destroyed. One after another, new bases were built, for air force, army, navy and marines—runways, hangars, training centers, ammo dumps, schools, PXs, theatres, gymnasiums, golf courses, coffee shops and barber shops and beauty shops and bowling alleys, motor pools and swimming pools, and mile after mile after mile of chain-link fencing, to keep the locals safely at a distance.

In 1972 we gave the islands back, and the Ryukyus once again became a southern prefecture. But we have remained, more visible here than in any other part of Japan. We have over forty military installations, the largest concentration anywhere outside the continental US. We lease and occupy about twenty percent of the island, one-fifth of the real estate. A big part of that is taken up by Kadena Air Base, the largest air base in the Pacific, the largest now in all of Asia.

Most local people would like to see it go away. Our days would be much quieter, they say, without the roar of your F-15s taking off and landing all the time. If the great base suddenly disappeared, they say, the island might lose some revenue, but our farmers and their animals would rest better at night. Life would be simpler and more harmonious without so many weapons of war right here in our own backyard, and the fact is, our architects and planners are already at work on other, safer ways to use all that military land.

While they say these things, and while they hope, they must know in their hearts that Kadena is not going to go away any time soon. The agreements that keep it and the other bases here are not made in Naha. They are made in

Tokyo and in Washington D.C. Not long ago the governor of Okinawa flew to Washington to share the concerns of his people with the appropriate committees on Capitol Hill. Among other things, they fear that the enormous military buildup will make them a target once again, if ever the shooting starts.

After the governor's visit, a congressional committee was appointed to fly out and look around. But it's doubtful that much will change. In Tokyo and Washington D.C. the general feeling seems to be that it's handy having all this firepower located three hundred miles or so from mainland China and within half an hour from North Korea, especially now that we've been ushered out of the Philippines, with Subic Bay and Clark closed down for good. On the Pacific Rim, this is our farthest outpost, our Fort Laramie.

FOOD AND DRINK

Our host is Katsunori Yamazato, a writer, a professor of English. He was born here, grew up in Naha, and remembers as a child looking through the fences at the wonders inside the American compounds—the tended lawns, the well paved roads, the big cars, sleek aircraft, buildings that always looked freshly painted. Compared to the world he was growing up in—a 1950s island world of cinder block housing and potholed roads, still recovering from the aftermath of the war—it was a fantasy land, so close, and yet so maddeningly out of reach. Is it any surprise that America would intrigue him and beckon?

Every professor we have met has studied in the States at one time or another. At Yale. At Stanford. Or the University of Georgia. Or the University of Kansas. The lines from Okinawa to the US run thick and deep.

"Do you know the city of Salinas?" a fellow says to us at a faculty reception.

"Yes, we know it well," Jeanne says. "It's only about twenty-five miles from where we live."

"I have visited Salinas several times. For the annual John Steinbeck festival."

Katsunori did graduate work in Honolulu, at the University of Hawai'i, and later at the University of California at Davis. He studied the writings of the poet Gary Snyder, who had found early inspiration in traditional Asian poetry, lived in Japan for a number of years, and found a transpacific voice, a way of speaking that joins the Far East with the Far West.

Katsunori has done something like this himself. He is bicultural now, and bilingual—or trilingual, if you include the Okinawan dialect. You could also say he is tricultural, since he knows all three of these histories, all three of the places that have shaped his life and his outlook.

A citizen of Japan, educated in the United States and a specialist in American literature, he is first and foremost a native of this island world his people have inhabited for centuries. The first thing we do, a couple of hours after checking into the hotel, is go out to a little restaurant that serves a kind of food he's proud of. As Jeanne has often observed, "Asia begins in the kitchen."

It has half a dozen tables, a purposely rough-hewn quality, a low ceiling supported by thick varnished logs. The cups and dishes are by a local potter, with a grainy texture that is comforting to touch. The tape loop is local too, thank god, a sound that is actually *of* this region—stringed instruments that sound a bit like banjo and fiddle, both plaintive and playful, backing a folk song.

We sit on the floor and begin to sample the food that appears in small bowls and saucers, dipping in with the chopsticks. Okinawan tofu is thicker, more textured than you see it in most of Japan. They raise a variety of taro here, which comes sometimes sliced in purple chunks, like potato, sometimes mashed and lightly fried, like a dumpling, seasoned with fish sauce and mushroom. There is rice in a sauce of mushroom and seaweed, and a bittermelon soufflé, and sea urchin served in little orange strips. You lay one on a small sheet of black seaweed, add wasabi sauce, a few strands of alfalfa sprout, fold over the seaweed, and dip an end into the soy sauce before you take a bite of this delicate Okinawan burrito.

Katsu has also ordered *awamori,* the local version of rice whiskey. It reminds me of sake, with a similar light, dry edge, but mustier. We sip it cold, from little ceramic saucers, each one holding an ice cube. Katsu says that newlyweds can go into a store and buy an earthenware jar of awamori and drink a ceremonial drink to commemorate their union, then leave the jar there with the storekeeper, who holds it with their name attached.

"Twenty years later," he says, "the couple can return and the storekeeper will find and open the same jar, and they can sip again, to celebrate their twenty years of happy married life. The jar is theirs forever, you see, unless of course the couple has split up somewhere along the way. In that case, the storekeeper gets to keep the jar."

Katsu says that when his son was born he bought a jar of awamori. He has it stored away. When his son turns twenty, he will open it and they will share a drink together.

Age is everything with awamori. When you order it in a restaurant, this is your first concern. You pay for the age. Ten years old? Twelve years old? The stuff he ordered here is twenty years old. He has a friend who keeps his best bottles buried under the house, digging them up only for special occasions. This fellow's best bottles have been around for forty years, fifty years.

There is a glint in Katsu's eye when he tells these stories, and it is not a drinker's glint. Something local is going on, something Okinawan. Awamori is often made with rice imported from Thailand, and this in itself has been no small feat, since importing rice into Japan has been so tightly controlled. During all the years that American rice merchants were banging on the gates, without success, Thai rice was allowed into Okinawa. Why? Katsu says it goes back to the days when this island was the center of the old Ryukyuan kingdom.

From the late fifteenth century onward, this was a maritime center, with many trading ships based in the harbor that borders one edge of Naha city. They carried raw silk and porcelain from China, swords and copper from Japan, sugar and spices from the islands farther south. Their cargo also included influences from all these directions, which the Ryukyuans blended into a crossroads culture that was uniquely their own.

Awamori, for example, is made by a process learned long ago from the Thai. The use of Thai rice is thought by some to be essential, and a good deal of pride is attached to the process and to the special dispensation that has allowed this rice to be imported. It is a link to that earlier time when Okinawa could be described as the Venice of the East.

GREAT
LEWCHEW
DISCOVERED

Twenty minutes to kill, waiting for a ride, in the lobby of the Dai-Ichi Hotel, in the Asato district of Naha City. It's like no other hotel I've seen in Asia, except perhaps for the Raffles in Singapore, which has a grander and more famous kind of bric-a-brac and cross-cultural assemblage of Pacific stuff.

Hotel is really too large a word. *Inn* comes closer, two floors of rooms, with a lobby that is part curio shop, part museum. On one side, floor-to-ceiling windows let in light from a small interior garden where leafy plants flourish and where the manager keeps her collection of ceramic *shisa,* the bearded, scowling lion-dogs who guard all the houses here. There are many dogs on Okinawa, but no one remembers any lions. The hybrid creature arrived, many centuries ago, from China. You usually see them perched on roofs.

Light spills in upon her shelves of local pottery, bowls and plates and small cups for sipping awamori, kept behind glass doors. On a broad, heavy table where breakfast is served each morning, there is a ten-foot length of the treasured fabric called *bingata,* cotton tinted with vegetable dyes, akin to Javanese batik. Bingata artists use rice starch rather than wax to shape the designs, and apply a mix of tree sap and soybean juice to prevent fading. This piece is very old, very elegant, rich indigo, crimson, dusky orange, protected by a table-wide pane of glass.

On a nearby chair sits an incongruous Mickey Mouse doll, the size of a small child, next to a tall grandfather clock that could be as old as the bingata cloth, old and European-looking and keeping good time, chiming when it should. The hands move at about the same altitude as the TV monitor, mounted above the door to the kitchen, which brings in a local news channel and game show chatter, the voices trickling down across Philippine round-back chairs of woven rattan, and two old-time T-shaped telephone stands, circa 1910, with the receivers curved like inverted candelabra. If you take a call in the lobby, you use one of these phones, passed across to you by the genial manager who gets a big kick out of herself and this eccentric headquarters where she spends most of her time.

She seems to be running the place alone. There is no man around. She speaks no English. So we bow a lot. We also laugh a lot. I point at something, and raise my eyebrows, and she points back. She has a survivor's kind of poignant, all-embracing laugh. She looks old enough to remember the war and the hard years after the war. The turn of her mouth, the bend of her brow tells you she has seen just about everything. Yesterday two of her grandkids were here, and they all sat by the dining room table, leaning on the glass pane that covers the old and irreplaceable length of bingata cloth, watching TV cartoons.

Opposite the big clock, on a low table next to this sofa, there is a stack of Japanese travel and fashion magazines, and some photo books of various ages. I pull out one called *Great Lewchew Discovered: Nineteenth-Century Ryukyu in Western Art and Illustration.* I start flipping through, not at all pre-pared to be startled by another incongruity.

This is a book of prints and drawings by European and American visitors whose ships landed here a hundred, two hundred years ago. Unlike Japan, the Ryukyuan kingdom never closed its doors to western traders and travel-ers. For centuries it was a place known for its hospitality and gentleness of spirit. The Chinese called it "the Nation of Constant Courtesy." The book shows scenes of village life and city life, the open look of Naha's streets, the open-air houses, the robes, the coiffures, men smoking under trees, women dancing, peasant dress, courtly dress.

Each page is a window into how things used to look, a nice little trip back into pre-modern times, and I am floating with it, dreaming with it, when the spell is suddenly broken by a small map that shouldn't be there—a map of the state of California, with one feature named and marked in bold outline.

It is the large chunk of land called Kern County, at the lower end of the great Central Valley, a county I happen to know fairly well. I have visited the place dozens of times, have friends in Bakersfield, and in fact have written a couple of articles about Kern County. But what is it doing in the middle of this book of scenes from the old Ryukyuan kingdom? Kern is as far from Okinawa as any two places can possibly be, in miles as well as in style. Much of it is the silted bottom of an ancient inland sea, where alkaline soil eats away at croplands, a flat, dusty realm of cotton rows and oil preserves. Not long ago Kern was producing more oil than some of the OPEC nations.

Around the tiny map, two facing pages show some watercolors and sketches done by one Edward Meyer Kern back in the 1850s, while he was a ship's artist on the U.S.S. *Vincennes,* with the Navy's North Pacific Exploring Expedition. The drawings are good, from the school of accurate and tasteful record keeping that preceded the advent of photography. One is called *Lew Chew Priests.* Another, *Chinese Ambassador's House: Road to Shuri.*

The small-print text tells me Kern's ship arrived here in November 1854, by way of Hong Kong, which would have been the year after Commodore Matthew Perry's famous entry into Tokyo Bay. Perry's mission was to pressure Japan to trade with the west. The job of the North Pacific Exploring Expedition was less confrontational, but equally significant in those first years of US expansion westward across the Pacific. They were out here to map and document the trading routes themselves, the sea-lanes to Japan and China, the reefs, the ports, the look of the shorelines.

And there was Edward Kern with his sketchpads and his paints, like a documentary filmmaker, taking it scene by scene. He has to be the same fellow I was reading about not long ago, the man Kern County was named for. In the 1840s he had come west from Philadelphia, crossed the continent on horseback with the third party led by Captain John C. Fremont. On that trip Kern was an artist too, as well as a topographer. Unofficially a conquistador,

Fremont claimed to be on a scientific quest, out to chart the as-yet-uncharted. The drawings and sketches Kern brought back provided some of the best early images we have from the American West before heavy settlement began.

He also figured in California's notorious Bear Flag revolt, the seizing of Sutter's Fort, and other rough-and-ready events leading up to the transfer of power from Mexico to the United States. Early in 1846, while passing through the Sierra Nevada range, Kern and a small detachment miscalculated a rendezvous point with the main Fremont party, and they spent three weeks waiting on the banks of the wrong river. Fremont—compulsive namer of natural features—later named that river after Edward Kern. Since the river happened to flow through most of the land that would become the county, one thing led to another. And that explains it. Kern was there for a while. Then he was here, drawing pictures.

But still . . .

It seems very strange, almost surreal, to be sitting on a sofa in Naha, in this hotel lobby with its collage from China and Manila and Okinawa and Hollywood, thinking about a fellow who once steamed out of Chesapeake Bay with the North Pacific Exploring Expedition and stopped here to draw a picture of Shuri Road, which I walked on just this morning—not very many blocks away. It is strange to spend a moment in this traveler's time warp, thinking of Edward Kern on the day he stopped by the wrong river, among mountains that were still part of Mexico, stopping for three weeks by the river now named for him, not only the river, but a town too, and a lake, and a major oil field, and a county that is somewhat larger than the state of Massachusetts.

And here is that county, depicted in *Great Lewchew Discovered.*

And here is that old watercolor Kern produced, of the Chinese Ambassador's house as it looked a hundred and forty years ago.

And who could have foreseen, when those Pacific-opening fleets stopped here in 1853 and '54—to bargain, to chart a trade route—that we would one day come back to occupy, and then to stay.

BY-LINES

On large maps you can barely see them curving through the East China Sea, this sprinkling of isles and islets, rocks and rocklets. Most of the names end in *-jima,* which means "island."

Ie-Jima is one of them, an offshore hump, just a ferry ride from Motobu Peninsula. There's a town out there, an airstrip, a pleasant swimming beach, and a memorial to one of those who fell during the days when it was the scene of heavy fighting. He was not a soldier. He was a writer, the popular war correspondent who won prizes for the stories he'd been sending back, stories that humanized the combat zone and made him a living legend, since it was clear from his intimacy with the troops that he was right there with them in the line of fire.

The shoreline monument says simply,

> At this spot the 77th Infantry
> lost a buddy, Ernie Pyle, 18 April 1945

His jeep was hit by mortar fire. I remember hearing about it, reading about it, when I was a kid. From the way grownups reacted, you could tell this came as a greater shock than the scale of the battle itself. Ernie Pyle was more than an intimate voice and compassionate witness. He had survived so many close calls, in earlier campaigns in Africa, Sicily, France, he had acquired a kind of saintly quality. He was perceived as a pure spirit. He had to be bullet proof.

He is buried in Honolulu, at the National Cemetery of the Pacific, inside the crater called Punchbowl. To this day, they say, his grave is the single most visited spot in the Hawaiian Islands.

Long before it became an American cemetery, the crater was a place of high ritual, a sacred place. Its Hawaiian name is *Pu'u Waina. Pu'u* means hill. *Waina* refers to offering or sacrifice. It is filled with the graves of those who died in our Pacific wars, in Korea, in Vietnam. You can wind your way through residential neighborhoods that climb toward the crater's walls and drive down inside and find Pyle's grave.

Think of Ernie Pyle. Born in Indiana in 1900. Killed on Ie-Jima at the age of forty-four. Buried in Hawai'i inside an old volcano where 22,000 memorials are laid out in white rows across the grassy floor.

VOICES

Until 1945, for most Americans, the name itself did not exist. The war gave "Okinawa" a ring. But the place, this long strip of land, was still remote, another distant battlefield. Then a play opened on Broadway, in October 1952, called *The Teahouse of the August Moon*. Enter Sakini, the first Okinawan in the history of American theater. Perhaps the first Okinawan in the history of theater anywhere outside the Ryukyus and Japan.

He is a bit of a rascal, a bit of a trickster, a crafty survivor in the days right after World War II. As the play unfolds he is also a voice of local wisdom.

"Country that has been invaded many times," he says in act 3, "soon master the art of hiding things."[7]

I brought the play along for in-flight reading. I'm sure now that I'll use it in my talk, "Asian Characters in American Writing," which looks at some of the ways characters of Asian background have been portrayed during the past hundred years or so. The Villain. The Available Female. The Immigrant. The Corporate Warrior (our Villain for the '90s). Sakini probably qualifies as a Wisdom Figure, of which there have been several, including another famous Okinawan, Mr. Miyagi, the shrewd martial arts mentor in *The Karate Kid* (1984), *The Karate Kid II* (1986), and *The Karate Kid III* (1989).

Right there you can see a big difference between the 1950s and the 1980s. White actors made Sakini famous—David Wayne on Broadway, Marlon

Brando in the 1956 film version. Mr. Miyagi was played by Pat Morita, and the part brought him an Academy Award nomination for Best Supporting Actor.

What's more, Mr. Miyagi has a history that adds to the story's emotional weight. Sakini has a personality, but he has no past.

Think of Miyagi, born in a village here, learned fishing and karate from his father, then immigrated to Hawai'i, as have thousands of Okinawans. In Hawai'i he met his wife, and they moved on to California in time to be interned at Manzanar. Leaving his pregnant wife behind, Miyagi volunteered for the draft. He joined the Japanese-American 442d Combat Regiment, the most decorated unit of World War II. He fought in Europe, earning medals for bravery. But while he helped the US win the war, both his wife and their baby were lost during childbirth inside the California internment camp.

Forty years later, as *The Karate Kid* reveals, the grief he still carries is transmuted into an affection for young Daniel, a teenage newcomer to the L.A. suburb where Miyagi now lives alone. The old warrior takes Daniel under his wing, teaching him the survival skills he needs to prevail over the local bullies who have it in for him.

The Teahouse of the August Moon is set in an Okinawan village in 1946, thus within a year or so after the largest combined air/sea/land battle in the history of warfare. But you would hardly know it from watching the play or the film. No one mentions the battle. What we know is that the war is recently ended, the village economy needs to be revived, and US Army occupation forces are here to supervise. Sakini is bilingual, an army interpreter, and principal spokesman for his home village of Tobiki. He has no personal story to tell. We don't know what he did before or during the war, or what his father or his family did. He has no wife, no children. In this family-centered society he has no relatives he mentions. Are they alive? Or dead? We don't know. As a survivor of that holocaust, he surely lost someone. But this isn't part of the play. John Patrick's script tells us he is "an Okinawan who might be any age between thirty and sixty. In repose his face betrays age, but the illusion is shattered by his smile of childlike candor."

I think *childlike* is the key word there, much in keeping with the way Sakini and the other villagers are portrayed. He is boyish, a floater, a free spirit, wise in his asides to the audience, adolescent in manner, a Puck for the seriocomic confusions of Captain Bisby, the American officer in charge of the village recovery program. The villagers are played this way too—happy-go-lucky, playful, easy to please.

This is a comedy, of course, a very successful one, winner of a Pulitzer Prize for drama in 1953. But still, looking back upon the time of the play's action, bearing in mind what had so recently occurred—the deaths of three to four thousand people per day every day for nearly three months, with the resulting destruction of almost everything that had held their lives and their island together—the play seems grotesquely lighthearted.

You can call it comedy. You can call it denial. You can also call it a sign of the times. 1952 was still too soon for actors of Asian background to be cast in major roles; and it was still too soon for most Americans to be looking at the full costs of the war. You might say that in 1952 it was a miracle for such a play to be produced at all—a bilingual production, with dialogue in both English and Japanese, with an Asian character in a leading role, and an Asian we are actually allowed to *like,* rather than encouraged to mistrust, which had been the norm in film and fiction, from the days of the Gold Rush onward.

Maybe, in the end, in that big void of What Is Not Yet Being Looked At, there is a core of sad truth. Maybe Sakini is like my wife's brother, Woody, who fought in the South Pacific during World War II and never talked about it after he came home. He found that he could make good money playing his comic role as valet to the wrestler, Mr. Moto, and he kept his wounds to himself.

It brings to mind the long silence of those who survived the wartime internment. Jeanne had to wait a quarter of a century before she could talk it through and finally tell the family's story, in *Farewell to Manzanar.* In a way she was speaking for her mother and father, who would not talk about those years. Thousands more have kept their silence to this day, leaving it to their children and grandchildren to act out what they cannot express, to release the deeper realms of feeling about that time and those places.

During the Redress and Reparations hearings in the 1980s, many older Japanese Americans came forth for the first time, to utter what had been, until then, unvoicable. A hearings commission was instructed by Congress to determine whether or not an injustice had been done to those interned, and whether or not the United States government was in any way at fault. As the commission moved from city to city, former internees stepped up to the microphone to testify. There is a powerful poem by Janice Mirikitani, written when her mother appeared at the hearing in San Francisco. It is called "Breaking Silence." After forty years the mother finds her voice; at the same time, the poet daughter is paying tribute to her pain and her courage.

> My mother
> soft like tallow,
> words peeling from her
> like slivers
> of yellow flame,
> her testimony
> a vat of boiling water
> surging through the coldest
> blue vein.

A page later in this three-page poem, the mother speaks before the hearing commission:

> Words are better than tears,
> so I spill them.
> I kill this, the silence . . .[8]

Maybe the words Sakini does not say, as of 1952, tell us something about a generation of Okinawans who have not yet spoken all that is in their hearts. Katsunori tells me there are numerous old-timers here who survived the battle but still haven't talked about what they witnessed or what they felt. He also says there are many others now, like Janice Mirikitani, looking for ways to help their elders break those silences.

THE VIEW
FROM SHURI

The district around the castle is still called Shuri Town. It's impossible to see where Shuri ends and the next town begins. Like San Jose and Los Angeles, communities have sprawled and merged to become Naha City (population 300,000 plus and growing), the packed capitol at the southern end of the island, facing west toward China.

The castle dates back to the twelfth century, built and rebuilt and added to as the years went by. After the First Sho Dynasty subdued their various adversaries and gained command over all these islands, Shuri Castle became the headquarters of the Ryukyuan kingdom. During the next five centuries it came to be known as one of the loveliest castles in Asia. Here the Chinese ambassadors were entertained. Here Commodore Matthew Perry was received in the spring of 1853, before the famous showdown at Tokyo Bay. Here Edward Meyer Kern and the officers of the U.S.S. *Vincennes* passed through a portal "for receiving the gods," and were greeted with smoking pipes and tobacco and tea.

The hilltop commands a panoramic view of green lowlands beyond the city, and blue ocean bordering the green. The castle itself is red and white, with a sine wave roofline over the main entry. Pillars gleam with the red you see in lacquerware. Walls and long stairways are so white you can't look at them in midday without dark glasses, stairs and parapets of fitted limestone as white as snow. Red pillars. Courtyards. Tiers of tiled roofing. Inside it is red and gold and black. Gold dragons wrap around posts of lacquered red. Black floors are lacquered to such a high polish they reflect the walls, the posts, the red border of the royal dais like a dark smooth lake of breezeless mountain water.

They say this castle's complete destruction in 1945 was one of the great architectural losses of the war, of the century. But here is where Japan's generals had established a military headquarters. The hill under the castle was their nerve center, an almost impregnable network of bunkers and corridors, extensions of a natural cave.

For years this hilltop was empty, a scorched reminder of the deadly battle, as well as the symbol of what it cost the Okinawan people—not only the loss of so many lives, but the loss of these invaluable chunks of history and cultural memory. With the demolition of the public buildings went all the public records. With the libraries went a multitude of books. With the destruction of homes and households went heirlooms and artifacts beyond number. After the smoke cleared, it was discovered—one small discovery, among thousands—that only two practitioners of the ancient textile art of *bingata* had survived.

Today you can once again visit the castle. You can stand here on the parapet and gaze out across the island, turn and contemplate the spacious courtyard striped red and white, the gracious limestone entry stairs—an exact replica of the way it looked for so many centuries. The recent completion of this new/old castle has had high symbolic importance, another sign of a past reclaimed, an identity reemerging.

From a parapet at one edge of the courtyard, gaze north across the city toward shoreline reefs. You can see the terrain covered by our army and marine divisions as they pushed south from the landing beaches. From another wall you can see portions of Haebaru, the district we visited last night. The island's southern end, where the Japanese were dug in so deeply, is still where most people live. The fighting in and around and above the towns like Haebaru went on for days and weeks. Jeanne and I were taken to the community center there, for a concert of traditional Ryukyuan dance, or so we thought. Before the musicians were set up, before the dancers made their entrances, there was time to look at the World War II exhibit.

This is what I need to write about. Or both of these together. The elegant perfection of the dance. And the somber artifacts. It is like the feeling up here at Shuri Castle, the new and resplendent building that reminds us of what stood here for so long, now rebuilt on the hill still laced with tunnels and chambers. To this day, Katsu says, some of their openings have never been unsealed.

❦

Inside the community center, a cave has been reconstructed. Low rocky compartments are fitted out with metal cots, sparse medical supplies—a replica of the numerous caves that served as wartime hospitals for Japanese troops. This coral-built island is full of natural caves where the wounded lay, where soldiers fought, where thousands of families hid. Near the coast, a few miles south of here, is the famous cave of Himeyuri, sometimes called "The Virgins' Cave," where 120 young women lost their lives. They were students from the local girls' high school and a teachers' training school, working as a nurses corps, and trapped in the cave by US flamethrowers and grenades. Some say that Japanese soldiers prevented their surrender. Some say it was another form of suicide, that their fear of Americans was greater than their fear of death.

On a long wall near the reconstructed cave there are three maps of the town of Haebaru, as it was laid out in 1945, street by street, house by house. On one map, about one-third of the houses are colored red. These are the houses in which all family members were killed during the fighting. On the next map, red marks the houses in which half the family members were killed. A third map marks the houses where one family member was killed. Every house in the town is marked on one of these three maps. And there are other maps like these, in other towns and districts, along with monuments and memorials by the hundreds, on this island where 160,000 civilians died during the eighty-two-day siege.

I'm still trying to comprehend such numbers. They never tell the story, or even come close. But maybe giving a moment to the numbers can be a way of beginning to acknowledge the enormity of what happened here. In terms of lives lost this was by far the costliest campaign of the Pacific war. In the battle for Saipan, 2,400 Americans died. In the battle for Iwo Jima, 7,000 died. The battle for Okinawa was in another league of slaughter.

American military losses: 12,500
Japanese military losses: 110,000
Okinawan civilian losses: 160,000

"You might wonder why so many died," said a fellow standing next to us in front of the maps, as we waited for the auditorium doors to open. His voice was level and matter-of-fact, a young professor from the university. "I'll tell you why. The generals had orders to hold the Americans here as long as possible, to prolong the fighting, so forces on the mainland could get ready for the American invasion they knew was coming next. That is why it went on so long. After a while they knew it was hopeless here. They could have surrendered and saved many many lives. But their orders were to buy some time, to fight to the death. So they sacrificed Okinawa."

It brings to mind Bikini Atoll, in the Marshall Islands group, south and east of here, which we sacrificed a year later, in 1946, to test an atom bomb. Not very many lives were involved. A couple of hundred. But a cultural history was involved. An ecology. The place is still uninhabitable. A way of life there was torn apart, in the name of military readiness.

For centuries now, like enormous sharks, the global players have moved back and forth through these waters. How many islands and islanders have been caught in their jaws like plankton?

ᗊ

The main hall of the community center had been set up with rows of folding chairs, facing a low platform. The musicians came out first, bearing instruments that told a story—round *taiko* drums, a flat *koto* with its movable frets, two banjo-shaped *sanshin* to play the lead, pick the melody line. The koto was introduced from Japan around 1700. The sanshin has been here much longer, since the fourteenth century, they say, brought over from China. It has three strings, a narrow neck, its head traditionally covered with snakeskin.

Two nights ago, at another, smaller gathering, we met a poet who had brought along one of these to pluck while he sang a few songs after dinner. According to him, the sanshin itself contains the pan-Asian quality of Okinawan culture. The neck was made of teak from Indonesia. The pick was from the Philippines, from a *carabao* horn. Strings were made of Chinese silk. The snakeskin top came from Thailand, while the body was of a locally grown mulberry, and the music the sanshin made, after six centuries, was Okinawan too. The single-string plucking sometimes has the driving insistence of a gamelan orchestra. The voices, singly or in unison, have echoes from China and India, as well as from Japan.

It's like the awamori, which can be compared with sake, yet is *not* sake. Just as the dancers, when they finally step out from behind the screens and take the stage, can be compared with Japanese dancers, but something different is going on, something *of* these islands.

It's hard to pin down. I am not a choreographer. The first dance is stately and reserved. The faces of the four women show no expression, as if covered with skintight masks. Their eyes move, but never blink. Eye movement is part of the intensely controlled pattern of the dance; and through that control, a high charge is released, a galvanic energy. I see Indonesia in this dancing. The planting of the feet, the slow circular turns, the delicate footwork seem both Japanese and Balinese.

This blend is in the costumes too. In the opening, welcoming dance, the women wear bamboo hats set high on the head, curving like umbrellas. They carry bamboo strips which they beat in time to the music. They wear robes that look very Japanese, yet the fabric and design is Okinawan bingata, with its echo of batik.

This troupe is said to be Okinawa's best, in the vanguard of the cultural revival here. They have traveled to the States, to perform in Honolulu and in Los Angeles. The musicians and dancers are trained and focused. You can see the commitment in every move. It's a youthful group, but you have the sense that they are working in a long tradition and know it and take great pride in keeping these dances alive. Some of them come from courtly days, when the king and his retinue still occupied the castle. Some come from the outer islands, fishing village dances, with peasant trousers and paddles in hand. There are harvest dances, stories of love, and unrequited love.

The program is long and full and varied, and before it's over, something unexpected happens, unexpected by us, that is, reminding us where we are—out here on an island, very close to the Tropics, where formalities can only go on for so long before you have to let your hair down. After the applause, after the dancers take their bows, the woman who is the leader beckons to the crowd. Suddenly chairs are scraping back.

"What now?" I say to Katsu.

"Kachashi," he says. "We often do it after a performance."

"Kachashi?"

"We do it whenever people get together and feel happy. Kachashi means everything mixed up. Just do anything you feel like doing."

This evening is not over until everyone joins in. The drum is drumming again, the koto is pinging, the sanshin is plinking and plunking. In the Haebaru Center, across the corridor from the wall of red-dotted maps, we are all hopping around the room, hands overhead, grinning and swinging and swaying, Jeanne and I and Katsu among the dancers, the coat-and-tied professors, the visitors, the people from town.

〽

From Shuri Hill, look out across the city. See the mountains to the north, the coral-bordered coastline, battlefields overgrown with almost fifty years of crops and grasses. On the roofs and in the yards, see the guardian lion-dogs called *shisa*. Taste the Thai rice that becomes awamori. Feel the bingata cloth. Hear the F-15s taking off from Kadena, *buh-room, buh-room*. Hear the plinking sanshin from China. And think about Kachashi, the dance that allows no spectators. Think about this new castle built upon the ruins, with tunnels of history still buried down below.

PACIFIC
KINGDOMS

So much here reminds me of Hawai'i. The archipelago itself.
The stories of ships, and of trade from all directions. The coral reefs. The
coco palms. The bougainvillea. Papaya and banana trees. The sugar cane.
The taro. Spring and fall the air is balmy. Sultry in the summertime, they say,
too sultry. Sticky. Like Honolulu, I imagine. There is an islander's personality too, hospitable, with a ready smile, ready to have some fun, to take a drive
around the island, to dance. In both places, dancers are bearers of the cultural
flame.

Like Hawai'i, this used to be a separate kingdom. It had its inequities, as
kingdoms always do, its human imperfections. But it was theirs. They had a
language, a royal lineage, a reputation as prosperous traders. The Japanese
began to penetrate in 1609, during what is called the Satsuma Invasion
(Satsuma, now a district of Kyushu, was still a southern fiefdom). Okinawa
was not taken over politically until 1879, after the Meiji Restoration. The new
regime annexed the Ryukyus and abolished the kingdom. It was a brutal and
greedy move, they say. But our own history in the Pacific makes it hard to be
judgmental.

Fourteen years later, in 1893, American military and business interests
took control of the Hawaiian Islands by force, ousting Queen Lili'uokalani
and bringing to an end the government of Hawai'i by Hawaiians. The island
chain was soon declared to be a territory of the United States. No one had

asked the queen or the Hawaiian people if they wanted their islands to be annexed. We just decided to take control.

In both cases, local language was suppressed in favor of the colonizer's language, and local culture was suppressed in favor of the colonizer's culture. New and similar legends rose up about both groups of islanders. They were lazy, stupid, backward, undercivilized. Okinawans and Hawaiians learned how to feel like second-class citizens in their own homelands.

Meanwhile, in both places the most populous islands were transformed into fortresses, strategically crucial, so that both Oʻahu and Okinawa became major flashpoints. The bombing of Pearl Harbor by Japanese pilots opened the Pacific war. The demolition of Okinawa very nearly brought the war to a close.

Today, in both places, a resurgence of cultural pride is in the air, and it is fed or sharpened or brought into sharper definition by this long experience with the military.

Consider the Hawaiian island of Kahoʻolawe, which has come to symbolize what was taken from the indigenous people. From 1942 onward it was used as a bombing and gunnery target, off-limits to all but US army and navy personnel. In 1976 a small band of Hawaiian activists crossed the eight-mile channel from Maui and landed on the island, to challenge the ruling and draw public attention to the fact that this island, once a human habitat and still the home of many sacred sites, had been bombed and strafed nearly to death. In the formative years of what is now called the Hawaiian Cultural Renaissance, "Protect Kahoʻolawe" became a rallying cry. After a few years of pressure, the Navy granted limited access so that old ceremonial sites could be restored. The pressure increased, until finally, reluctantly, they agreed, in 1990, to stop the bombing and let the island heal.[9]

〰

The Ryukyuan kingdom had no military. It was a little world without weapons. Karate was developed here, they say, as an alternative to bearing arms. (*Kara-te.* The two characters for this word literally mean "empty hand.") From the Okinawan point of view, it was the Japanese buildup that led to the island's destruction. "We had no enemies then," we heard some-one say last night, "the Japanese had enemies."

Today they look at the bases that never go away, and they see another form of that same danger. All these weapons, all these missiles, all these bombs and planes and ships—isn't this the very reason Okinawa had to be attacked back in 1945?

Two nights ago we heard a man read a poem about the long legacy of that war. He talked about what it's like to visit the cliffs along the southern shore where so many civilians took their lives, where their spirits still linger. As on Saipan, but in greater numbers, they leaped rather than risk capture by the Americans they'd been told would rape and torture them. This poet was not angry or out for revenge. But he wanted us to know that these things had happened, to somehow begin to know what his island has felt, what his part of the world has had to absorb. He is passionate with a long-term grief and passionate to somehow reclaim or re-own the history of his homeland; this in itself would be a kind of tribute to the family members he personally has lost.

By day this poet teaches high school chemistry. By ten o'clock at night the stubble of a heavy beard had started to show across his cheeks and chin, making his swarthy skin swarthier. He has straight black hair, eyes dark and round. In another setting he would look Italian.

There were eight of us around a table in a private room at a small restaurant when he pulled a headband out of his coat pocket and wrapped it across his forehead and tied it behind, white cotton with blue diagonals. He stood up and read his poetry in three languages, in the English translation a friend had done for him; then in Japanese; then in the Okinawan dialect, which he afterward talked about with relish and pride, the way a Welsh poet I once traveled with would talk about the Celtic sounds that gave Wales its own brand of poetic music. Words you wouldn't hear in Japan are part of an older Okinawan speech, as well as the use of certain consonants, such as *P* and *F*. There are other variables in pronunciation, and something about the dialect itself requires the voice to soften.

He reminded me of Hawaiians I have met who are teaching their children to speak the native tongue in spite of those who ask, "What good will it do your kids when they have to earn a living and get along in the world?" These fathers and mothers reply, "What good will it be to make a living in the world if our children forget who they are as Hawaiians, if they never know their history or feel it in their bones and in their blood? And where is the culture rooted, if not in the language we have almost let die away? It is right here in the throat and the old sounds vibrating through your body when you speak."

This is what I heard in the small room in the restaurant, in the voice of the chemistry teacher, the gentle-spirited and cultural patriot, as he read to us. All these things are connected—his voice was saying—the poem, the language of the poetry, the history of the Ryukyus, the terrible losses that must be looked at and remembered and not forgotten, yet be absorbed so that we can keep our strength and somehow cut a path between Japan and the United States and find the Okinawan way.

FROM THIS MOUNTAIN SHORE

VI

MONTEREY BAY, LOS PADRES, TASSAJARA

Here from this mountain shore, headland beyond
stormy headland plunging like dolphins through the
    blue sea-smoke
Into the pale sea—look west at the hill of water: it is
half the planet: this dome, this half-globe, this bulging
Eyeball of water, arched over to Asia . . .
        — Robinson Jeffers, "The Eye" (1948)

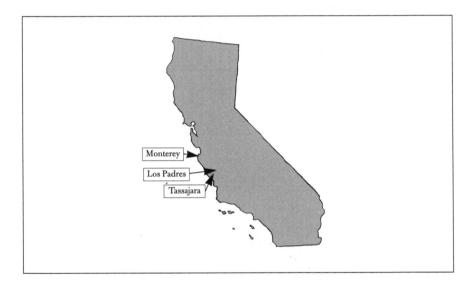

California, facing the Pacific.

STORY LINES

When the fog lifts and a good wind has cleared the air above the bay, I can see Monterey Peninsula, twenty miles away. On such a morning, after the wind falls off, the water turns to glass, and you can see faint edges of the communities that fringe the bay's curve. Above these towns the profile of ridges against the southern sky is actually one end of the Santa Lucia Range, which stretches south to Big Sur and beyond. This long and mostly uninhabited mountain system shapes the famous shoreline that takes its name from a river early explorers called El Rio Grande del Sur, "The Big River to the South."

They meant south of Monterey, which was for a while the main town of Mexican California. I have often wondered what might have happened if Santa Barbara had been chosen as the provincial capitol. With a different reference point, explorers might have named it "The Big River to the North," and we would now be calling that legendary coastline Big Norte.

So much depends upon your point of view, upon where you are standing, which way you are looking. And as it is for Big Sur, so it is for this entire edge of the continent.

When I first studied history, Europe was the reference point, and the great cities of Europe: Athens, Rome, Paris, London. Growing up in San Francisco I was trained to see California as a region defined by huge migrations west-

ward from Atlantic to Pacific. This coastline was perceived as the farthest edge and outer limit in a steady pattern of conquest and expansion and settlement that had begun in Europe in the late fifteenth century.

In those days it would never have occurred to me to examine this view, since it seemed to make perfect sense. If anything it explained and perhaps ennobled my own family's leapfrog history, my mother and father trekking west from Texas back in the 1930s, soon followed by my grandmother and a couple of uncles, all looking for a better life. This view was reinforced by numerous wagon train and cavalry movies and also by certain works of prose and poetry I came upon. In this region's literature it has been a prevailing view for two centuries and more, dating from the reports and diaries of the earliest missionaries and trappers.

From my upstairs window, looking south and east on a day such as this, I can see the outlines of what is sometimes still called "Steinbeck Country." Where the Santa Lucia Range slopes inland, the broad delta of the Salinas River spreads out to meet the bay. A few miles farther down that valley is where John Steinbeck set his short novel, The Red Pony. *It ends with a chapter called "The Leader of the People," about the grandfather in a Salinas Valley ranching family. This is a man who crossed the plains late in the nineteenth century. Some fifty years later he is spending his days filled with nostalgia and regret for where he has arrived. He is telling his grandson Jody what it was like to cross the plains:*

> *"It was a whole bunch of people, made into one big crawling beast. And I was the head. It was westering and westering. Every man wanted something for himself, but the big beast that was all of them wanted only westering. I was the leader, but if I hadn't been there, someone else would have been the head. The thing had to have a head.... The westering was as big as God, and the slow steps that made the movement piled up and piled up until the continent was crossed."*[10]

Jody the grandson dutifully listens, waits while the old man wipes his eyes, then wonders if he too might one day lead the people on such a trip. Granddad shakes his head.

> *"There's no place to go. There's the ocean to stop you. There's a line of old men along the shore hating the ocean because it stopped them."*

This view has been in the air for quite some time, the West Coast as the outer limit of something that began farther east. By the 1930s, when Steinbeck wrote The Red Pony, *and on into the 1960s, California was frequently described not only as the farthest edge but as a kind of end zone, a place where things had finally run their course. In Joan Didion's classic essay, "Notes From a Native Daughter," there is an oft-quoted passage that perfectly articulates the mid-'60s view:*

> *California is a place in which a boom mentality and a sense of Chekhovian loss meet in uneasy suspension; in which the mind is troubled by some buried but ineradicable suspicion that things had better work here, because here, beneath that immense bleached sky, is where we run out of continent.*[11]

What such a picture does not include are the waves of people who have reached these shores from other directions—from the south, and from the north, and from the east, across the water. When my wife's father arrived from Japan by way of Honolulu in 1904, this coastline was his point of entry into a land he had yet to explore.

Consider that scene in Maxine Hong Kingston's first book, The Woman Warrior (1976), *when the Chinese mother is waiting at San Francisco International Airport to meet a sister she has not seen in thirty years. On this day the mother has traveled from the Central Valley town of Stockton, where she has raised her American-born children and where her tales and superstitions and folk wisdom have had a great influence on the daughter/narrator. The name of the sister arriving from China is Moon Orchid. The mother, Brave Orchid, has arrived early, to work a benevolent spell:*

> *She had begun this waiting at home, getting up a half-hour before Moon Orchid's plane took off from Hong Kong. Brave Orchid would add her will power to the forces that keep an airplane up. Her head hurt with concentration. The plane had to be light, so no matter how tired she felt, she dared not rest her spirit on a wing but continuously pushed up on the plane's belly. She had already been waiting at the airport for nine hours.[12]*

What is going on here? A woman has family lines that stretch seven thousand miles across the ocean. In her mind she reaches out to help keep the plane aloft, to ensure a safe landing. For these sisters, San Francisco and south China are linked by air, by water, by ancestry, and by blood, and the western shore is not the last stop, or the end of the line. It is the first stop.

❧

In this big panorama of movement and migration, who then is the archetypal traveler? Is it the one who crossed the plains? Is it the one who crossed the ocean? Or might it be someone like the notorious Captain John Sutter, who apparently arrived here from both directions at the same time.

He is the one who founded Sutter's Fort, where Sacramento is located now. Before it became world famous, after the discovery of gold at Sutter's Mill on the American River in 1848, his fort was already legendary as the first haven for wagon trains that had made it through the Sierra Nevada. At the end of the long crossing, travelers knew that an outpost awaited them, where they could refresh their animals, replenish supplies, rest up a while and regroup before moving on to a final destination in the Promised Land.

It is a seldom-mentioned fact that Sutter reached California by way of Hawai'i and that several of his ranch hands were Polynesian.

In April 1838 he had set out from St. Louis and followed the Oregon Trail to the mouth of the Columbia River. Arriving in December, after the heavy weather had set in, he was advised to wait until winter rains were over before trying to move south. But Sutter was an impatient man, dreaming of ranches, so he caught a merchant ship for Hawai'i, hoping he would find there a ship bound for the bay of San Francisco. He had to wait four months. At last he secured a job as supercargo on a vessel heading back toward the West Coast.

In Honolulu he had hired ten Hawaiians to travel with him, eight men and two women, offering them three years' employment. Soon after they had sailed through what is now called the Golden Gate, he chartered a local schooner, and they all set out together from the tiny port town of Yerba Buena. They passed through the maze of delta islands and started north up the Sacramento River. Where it met the American, Sutter staked out his claim. It was August 1839.

The first buildings erected upon this historic site were not made of adobe. They were not log cabins. They were grass houses, pili hale, *built in the Hawaiian style by his crew of islanders. Sutter's common-law wife was Hawaiian too. Her name was* Manu-iki *("Little Bird"). She kept a vegetable garden there.*

Think of it! At the farthest border of the American frontier, a lone outpost is surrounded with tribal villages. California is still a northern province of Mexico. Captain John Sutter, an immigrant from Switzerland, has a girl-friend from the Hawaiian Islands. His first and most reliable ranch hands are from Hawai'i too. They have names like Kanaka Harry, Sam Kapu, *and* Maintop. *They stay with him for years.*

Once the fort was established, with walls and outbuildings and a couple of cannons, Sutter's link with the rest of the world was his launch, the Sacra-mento, *named for the river. It made regular runs to San Francisco Bay under the command of Maintop, who gave the broad waterway seasonal Hawaiian names. In winter he called it* Muliwai Konaoli, *"Turbulent River." In summer he called it* Muliwai Ulianianikiki, *"Dark Smooth Swift River."*

❧

Sam Kapu and Maintop weren't the first Pacific islanders to reach these shores.

The back-and-forth traffic that continues to this day had begun years earlier. Cook's third voyage had put Hawai'i on the nautical maps of the world. By the 1820s Hawaiians could be found on just about every ship bound for the Americas, sought out by the merchant fleets, to work the big trading triangle that linked Honolulu and Lahaina with Peru and Chile and the ports of Mexican California. As an island people they were exceptionally skilled in the water. They had their own two-thousand-year tradition of oceanic travel without instruments in double-hulled voyaging canoes.

Four years before Sutter's arrival, Richard Henry Dana had sailed up this coast, and he met Hawaiians at every stop. Some were on shore leave. Others were already bedded down to stay. In Two Years Before the Mast, *which provides one of the earliest detailed looks at the Pacific coast, he describes their songs, their voices, their wit, their loyalties:*

> *. . . they were the most interesting, intelligent, and kind hearted people that I ever fell in with. . . . I would have trusted my life and my fortune in the hands of any of these people.*[13]

Dana had left Harvard for medical reasons, had gone to sea, and had come around Cape Horn on a trading ship bound for California, in search of cattle hides. Their first West Coast stop was Santa Barbara. It was January 1835. Young Dana was in the first longboat trying to make the beach, and a heavy winter swell was running. The Americans were worried about capsizing in the shorebreak, when they were shown how to do it by the crew from another ship that had recently dropped anchor there. These were Hawaiian sailors, accustomed to moving canoes through rushing surf:

> *. . . they gave a shout, and taking advantage of a great comber which came swelling in rearing its head . . . they gave three or four long and strong pulls, and went in on top of the great wave, throwing their oars overboard, as far from the boat as they could throw them, and jumping out the instant that the boat touched the sand, and then seizing hold of her and running her up high and dry upon the sand . . .*

❧

It has always been a shoreline with a double edge—western border of the North American continent, which some geologists say was once, in eons past, joined physically to Europe; eastern rim of this circular ocean that touches Asia, the South Pacific, Polynesia, Alaska, and Mexico.

From here I can look south across the bay toward the Santa Lucia range. One slope faces the Salinas Valley. The other slope meets the sea. And it is all right there, where blunt headlands and their drop-off cliffs mark the edge with such spectacular finality, all in the air at once, all the things we have asked this part of the world to be, and wanted it to be, and claimed it to be, and often feared it would become.

Land of Promise.

Continent's End, and shipwreck beach.

The last stop.

The first stop.

Shoreline on a wheel of shores.

CULTURE
SHOCK

One more trip, another short one, an overnight retreat into the wilderness a couple of hours down the coast. Home again after the months overseas, we're both still restless, still in some kind of traveling mode that has to be spent, expended, and Jeanne is yearning for hot springs. After the long stay on Kyushu she is addicted to them now.

"The creek should be full," she says, "with all the rain I've heard about. They say the drought is over, at least for this year."

"Yes, all the creeks are full right now, the dams, the lakes. It's a good time to roam around and see some things."

We are speeding south along Highway 1, crossing Soquel Creek, Aptos Creek, the Pajaro River delta, following the half-moon of Monterey Bay past Watsonville, Moss Landing, Seaside, the coastal towns.

"I just wonder why everybody is roaming around on the same day."

"It's always like this," I say. "Maybe we've been away too long."

"It hits you in the face," she says.

"What? The traffic?"

"I can't put my finger on it. Maybe it's the feeling of the traffic."

"The impatience . . ."

"More than that," she says. "It's like a frenzy. You feel it as soon as you step off the plane. Everybody on a hair trigger, or challenging something. Is it worse now than when we left? It feels thick to me. So thick you could capture it in jars and use it like fuel. Look at that bumper!"

A sleek BMW has just whizzed past, with a sticker saying:

RUGBY PLAYERS EAT THEIR DEAD

"That's grotesque," she says.

"He's only kidding. It's just a figure of speech."

"But when that is typical, when you put a statement like that on the back of your car and drive around—doesn't it tell you something about a person's state of mind? There's another one!"

A pickup is rising on my left, a Bronco with deep-tread tires high enough for a diesel rig. Next to the door handle on the passenger side she has spotted a small warning to any would-be vandal:

INSURED BY SMITH AND WESSON

"Is that a figure of speech?" she says.

I glance at the driver, a burly fellow with wiry blond hair poking out behind the reverse bill of his ballcap.

"No," I say, "I think he means it."

"Touch his pickup and he could blow you away."

"Something along those lines."

"You'd never see anything like that in Fukuoka."

"You wish you'd stayed overseas?"

"Reentry is tough, that's all. You just forget what it's like. Things you sort of stopped paying attention to are suddenly . . . The whole atmosphere . . . I guess you forget what it *feels* like here."

"But you're glad you're back."

"Hey, six months is plenty."

She grabs my arm, scoots in closer. Her eyes are shining. She is still high on travel, still floating in the giddy limbo zone between shores, between tongues and time zones. "This is where we come from, isn't it?"

"The mountains will be different," I say.

"I know. I can't wait."

LISTENING

We follow the Carmel River inland, with tawny ridges hump-
ing above the condo clusters and white-railed corrals. The valley narrows to
a thickly wooded corridor, and then the semi-rural feel gives way to dry and
rolling open country. Twenty miles in we take a logging road south to the end
of the pavement, where we park our car and catch the mountain shuttle van,
a workhorse Ford with nine seats and four-wheel drive and many gears. They
call it "the Tassajara Stage," harking back to the days a hundred years ago
when a horse and wagon traveled three times a week over this same tortuous
fourteen-mile track.

Heading farther south, we climb past the scars of old fires, with blackened
limbs still poking through the newer growth, and here and there a tree trunk
split by lightning. The dust billows out behind, while the ridges roll away in
both directions, east toward the Salinas Valley, west toward the unseen
ocean, and no habitat visible now, just the gorges, the ribs of granite, and
slopes furred with live oak, pine, manzanita.

In low gear for the zigzag descent we drop from five thousand feet, honk-
ing on the blind curves, and arrive at last at a long dusty clearing lined with
dusty cars and pickups, and pull into the canyon/oasis where it's already hot,
a dry desert heat, though the canyon is green and the creek gushes through
it. The heat itself slows you down, says Take your time, take your time.

The cabin is simple, old redwood siding, with a double mattress on the

floor, two wooden chairs, a small chest of drawers, kerosene lamps, no elec-
tricity, screens for windows, or translucent plastic tarp, so the sound of the
creek, the dripping rush of it, is always there, indoors and out, all day and
night, contained and amplified within the canyon's narrow, rocky walls.

We change into the robes we picked up before the trip to Yufuin. Yukata
for me. Kimono for Jeanne. Geometrical patterns of blue on white, diagonals
and diamonds, sashes at the waist. Put the shoes away, step into slippers, and
shuffle along the swept path toward the bath house, passing other cottages
like the one we've rented, survivors from the days when this was a hunting
and fishing retreat. Now yellow-green bamboo rises next to some of the walls.
Reed fencing lines the path, and retaining walls of fitted stone. Small settings
of creek-rolled stones have been arranged next to the steps of the cottages,
giving each entryway the look of a little Japanese garden. Slippers and getas
have been left outside the doors.

Past the meditation hall, past the cookhouse, an arching bridge crosses
over the creek. An American trout stream. An Asian footbridge, made of carefully crafted, curving wood. At the far side a small altar is waiting, with incense sticks, a new blossom, a figure of the Buddha. We pause and bow,
which is a way of honoring that place in each of us where the universe resides,
the still center that links us all. This figure has found its way to the wilderness
creekside from India, by way of China, Japan, San Francisco—serene man
sitting with his feet in his lap and his hands folded. Not such a bad idea, that
kind of serenity. Not such a bad ideal. If you can get to it. Or close to it. If only
every once in a while.

The next step is down into the heat and steam piped up from the mineral
springs that have bubbled here for longer than anyone can remember, and
said to be the richest springs in the United States. In these waters thirty-two
minerals have been identified, among them sulfur, sodium, calcium, magne-
sium, potassium, iron. Drop the robe. Slide into the wide tub lined with tile.
This time of day I have the men's side to myself. Beyond the wall I can hear
women talking. Like the creek sound, their voices punctuate the stillness.
Don't move too much. Moving makes currents, and the scalding currents
hurt. Let the surface turn to glass. Smell rocks in the water, a faint sulfur whiff.

Heat to the neck. To the chin. As long as I can stand it. Then down a rocky path to the little reservoir of cold mountain water three feet deep, backed beyond the low stone dam. Plunge in and feel the fingerlings poking at my feet and legs, tiny fishlets come to investigate, darting in the cold cold creek.

Splash out, and head for tubs again, for more heat.

More cold.

More heat.

More cold.

Dry off. Slow down. At the altar, we bow again to the Buddha, and the little hand-lettered sign that sums it up:

> With all beings
> I wash body and mind
> Free of dust
> Pure and shining
> Within and without.

Walk back along the path, under a canopy of limbs and leaves, the granite walls rising, catching light.

Below the cabin, next to a creekside sycamore, someone has placed a battered chair, a weatherworn wooden chair that looks older than the cabins, and that is the place to sit a while and listen. No phones down here. No radio. No TV. No boom box from the guy in the next lane or from a garage across the way. No cars inside the compound. No ads. No neon. No e-mail or Internet or fax machine for urgent messages. Just this dry heat under oaks and sycamores, the steady tumble of the creek, the squawk of jays coming to see who's here and check for random scraps of food, with a breeze along the water from time to time to riffle leaves that send sparks of sunlight through the canyon shade. When the alder leaves quiver, a softer light splashes upward, mountain strobe light rippled by the creek god's hidden hand.

A MORNING
PILGRIMAGE

Waking early I hear the sound of water against the far wall of our cabin, like bacon sizzling on a grill. Jeanne will sleep until the chill is off the air and then head straight for the baths, to get in a soak before breakfast. I have a morning pilgrimage in mind, up to the spot where they've erected a memorial to the man who first imagined this old-time mountain resort could be transformed into a Zen retreat and monastery.

His name was Shunryu Suzuki Roshi. Born in Japan in 1905, he came to the US at the age of fifty-three. They say he was a small and very private fellow, both humble and forceful, instructing more by example than by words. He'd been trained in the Soto Zen tradition, and going to America was, for many years, his dream. When he was invited to become the priest at a San Francisco Buddhist temple, in 1958, he readily accepted. Before long he had founded the San Francisco Zen Center which, in 1967, acquired this acreage in Tassajara Canyon. It was the first Zen monastery to be established anywhere in the world outside Asia.

Four years later Suzuki Roshi passed away, having spent the final months of his life right here, gardening, lecturing, preparing himself and his followers for his death. In the style and feel of what this place has become, in the gardens, in the very joints of the carpentry, his example and his spirit live on.

Yesterday, in the office, I was checking through the shelf of books and pamphlets they keep for browsers, and I heard someone behind the counter say that after his cremation, his ashes had been divided, with some buried here and some buried in Japan. Though I've been to the canyon a dozen times, I'd never heard this mentioned. It took me by surprise, caused my forearm hairs to prickle.

"Dividing the ashes," I said, "that's quite a statement."

"He felt such strong ties to both places," this woman replied. She wore a collarless shirt, round glasses, brown hair cropped close.

"Do you know where in Japan?"

"Where he came from, I think. But I'm not sure about the details. You'd have to ask someone who's been around here longer than I have."

At this early hour the jays are quiet. Sutras spill from the zendo in low-voiced Japanese. When the voices fade behind me, there is only the creek. From the road I take a narrow footpath that begins a steady climb through live oak and bay and sycamore. A couple of switchbacks, another climb, then I pass below an overhang into a small clearing of raked gravel, under an umbrella of oak limbs, the kind of space that requires you to stop and pay attention. Someone has already been up here this morning. The tine marks look fresh. The ground itself says Walk with care.

A low retaining wall of fitted stones is built against the farther embankment. In front of it stands a chunk of granite about four feet high, roughly triangular, with a flat side facing out. The stone is gray with a greenish cast. From the top, a coating of white, like thick paint or white lava, seems ready to spill. A streak of white cuts across the flat face of the stone like a vein just under the skin, or a lightning streak. Where did it come from? I wonder. There is movement in this stone, an uncarved, unaltered piece of natural sculpture that is stationary and fixed, yet somehow catches and conveys the flow and energy of life.

Around it, smaller stones make an altar, where pale green mandalas of lichen cling. On the flat place in front of these stones, a metal vase holds a bamboo stem, some wildflowers, and next to it an incense bowl.

This slightly sculpted place has the feel of the garden we saw in Japan, behind the Zen temple at Dazaifu, outside Fukuoka, though it is more surprising, somehow more remarkable, since this little space has been cleared at the very edge of raw wilderness. Here and there, young trees rise through the gravel, so that the space is open yet not empty of vegetation. With its canopy of limbs it is in fact just one step away from the rugged terrain you see beyond the trees, the steep ridges higher up with their rocky outcroppings, the empty arroyos veering off through cliffs of scrub oak and manzanita.

The centerpiece, the quietly majestic hunk of living stone, is *of* that terrain, still connected to it, though set apart now, singled out, to honor the pioneering roshi. This shrine also honors and recognizes all that surrounds it here, the singularity of every other stone, each leaf, each life, each day, each bird trill in the morning air, each moment in the midst of the cosmic pond that has no beginning and no end.

HEADING
BACK

The Tassajara Stage sets out at about three each afternoon for its return trip through the mountains. I'm in the front seat next to the driver. Jeanne is farther back, sitting with a woman from Santa Cruz she hasn't seen in months. They met in the baths an hour and a half ago and have been chatting ever since, catching up.

The driver is a trim and bearded fellow, with a ready smile, easy to sit next to. He's comfortable with silence, yet talkative if it's time to talk. When he tells me he's been with the Zen Center for over twenty years, I see that he is the one I've been hoping to meet. I ask him if he knows where the roshi's memorial stone might have come from, and he says yes, he does. He describes the legendary day it was hauled up from the river bottom, back in 1973.

"They used a winch," he says. "It's local granite, right out of the canyon. So it hasn't gone very far at all."

"It must weigh seven or eight hundred pounds."

"Probably more. It was quite a task, took most of a day to get it up there in place on that little ridge where you see it now."

I ask him about the ashes, and he says, "It's true. They were divided between this place and his home temple."

"And where was that?"

"Near Yaizu, where his son is now the priest, a fishing town on the coast south of Tokyo, not far from where Suzuki Roshi was born. The temple is called Rinso-in."

"This had to be the roshi's wish," I say, "to be buried in both places."

"I'm sure it was. Long before he actually came here he felt that sooner or later his path would bring him to this country. He saw early on that the US would be the next beachhead for Zen. And in a broader sense I think he had for years seen the importance of Asia and America gradually moving closer together, not only in the economic and political realm, though that is always part of it, but in the human and the spiritual realm. So yes, it was right in line with his commitment."

Again, my arm hairs prickle at the thought of a man committing his ashes to the soils of two lands. As the van labors upward, we talk about the inspirational quality of such a gesture—quiet, personal, nonpublic, unadvertised. We talk about the eternal quest for union, in the face of the countless divisions that conspire against it and separate us one from the other. And we laugh at the irony here, that the separating of the roshi's ashes is a marvelous symbol of joining, linking, another kind of bridge across the water.

Then we stop talking for a while. Steep hairpin turns and the multiple gears require his full attention, with stretches of dusty road narrowed by washouts, and with glare across the windshield from the unobstructed sun. As we leave the canyon monastery far below, heading back toward Monterey, toward speedway traffic and the busy swirl, the higher peaks come into view, a sea of ridges swelling outward, slopes and creases of the long mountain system they call the Coastal Ranges. They run south from here to Santa Barbara, north to the Columbia.

This kind of country takes me back to the hot days my dad and I once spent together, years and years ago, in search of wild game, and also in search of something more primal, more essential. In search of some simplicity, some silence, the memory of wildness. The hunting and the bearing of rifles through terrain such as this was his way to get out of the city and feel the day's shadow come sliding down a burnished slope, to remember that these stands of oak and pine went on for miles and the land we had entered was as thick with wildness as the late-night sky was thick with stars.

As we near the crest, voices one by one fall silent. A few heads loll with drowsiness. The engine's grinding hum is like a narcotic inside the van, and like a mantra, to settle and release the mind. Our talk about bridges has started me thinking once again about a more recent time, about my last night on Bali, in the upcountry village of Ubud, where the sky, free of metro-glare, was also thick with stars.

I had come in late and found upon the edge of my porch a familiar plaited basket. It held a couple of flowers, a few grains of rice, drops of holy water. I knew who had placed it there. I'd been watching the young woman who brought the daily offerings to the shrines and to our bungalows. She worked there at Oka Wati's. She carried these tiny baskets in a larger basket made of straw. On each shrine there was a narrow shelf where the offerings were set. Sometimes she would light an incense stick.

Standing on the nighttime porch I felt that I was finally beginning to understand what Jelaluddin Rumi meant by people "going back and forth across the doorsill where the two worlds touch."[14]

The sounds of the gamelan, the baritone and alto gongs, the insistent drumming, all the shrines in all the family temples that line the roads through the villages, along with the ceremonial parades and the offerings upon my porch each day—all these gestures, these rituals large and small, were designed to keep you in the vicinity of that doorsill, on that threshold. Most of the Balinese I had met seemed to live right there. You could see it in their eyes.

In middle America you can live there too, but it's harder. It goes against the grain. We are trained to polarize the situation, to make it *them* or *us,* and either/or. Either you are a mystic, or you are a materialist. You are a nuts-and-bolts rationalist who believes in the microwave oven and the gross national product. Or you are a shaved-head chanter doing flower petal ecstasy and making it hard for sensible shoppers to get into the department store. Daily journalists will go out of their way to debunk or discredit spiritual leaders, while our culture heroes continue to be Arnold Schwarzneggar, Howard Stern, Madonna.

We also wrestle with this idea that a truly devotional or God-seeking person, someone who aspires to union or re-union with a higher power, must also renounce material attachments. This goes all the way back to the New Testament and beyond, and it has led to a divided attitude toward material well-being. If you happen to achieve some material well-being you must at some level have sold out to mammon, because you can only have one or the other. Either you renounce, or you compromise yourself.

According to Rumi there is a threshold where the two worlds touch. That night I saw how Bali's culture permitted you to stay on this threshold. I was grateful for the example, for the guidance, for the message still in the air around that ancient island.

We're talking about borderlands again. Not national or ethnic borders. Another kind. Something in the atmosphere that night said it is still possible to inhabit the borderland between . . . between? . . . Well, how would you describe these two touching worlds? What are we really talking about here? The material and the mystical? The practical and the mysterious? The flesh and the spirit? The known and the unknown? The outer and the inner?

Yes. Both of those.

All of those. Along with the male and the female. And the East and the West. That was the lesson I would have to carry back with me: depolarize, and strive to live your life at the touchpoint.

Fukuoka, Volcano, Santa Cruz
October 1995

Notes

1. T. S. Eliot, "Little Gidding," *Four Quartets* (New York: Harcourt Brace and World, 1944).

2. In November 1993, President Bill Clinton signed the Joint Resolution, authored by Senator Daniel Akaka, which acknowledged the illegal overthrow of the Kingdom of Hawai'i one hundred years earlier, and formally apologized to Native Hawaiians on behalf of the people of the United States.

3. Michael Crichton, *Rising Sun* (New York: Alfred Knopf, 1992).

4. James King, *A Voyage to the Pacific Ocean*, Volume III (London: G. Nicol and T. Cadell, 1784).

5. Ke'aulumoku, *'Au'a 'Ia*, ca. 1784. Translation by John Charlot.

6. Garcí Ordoñez de Montalvo, *The Adventures of Esplandian* (Seville, 1510). From the 1872 translation by Edward Everett Hale, reprinted as *The Queen of California* (San Francisco: Colt Press, 1942).

7. John Patrick, *The Teahouse of the August Moon* (New York: G. P. Putnam, 1952).

8. Janice Mirikitani, "Breaking Silence," from

Breaking Silence: An Anthology of Contemporary Asian American Poets, (Greenfield Center, NY: Greenfield Review Press, 1983).

9. Since then President Bill Clinton has signed a bill returning control of Kahoʻolawe to the state of Hawaiʻi (November 1993), with funds earmarked for clean-up of spent and unspent ordinance. The state legislature, in turn, has passed a bill designating the island as a cultural and historic preserve.

10. John Steinbeck, *The Red Pony* (New York: Covici-Friede, 1937).

11. Joan Didion, "Notes From a Native Daughter," from *Slouching toward Bethlehem* (New York: Farrar, Straus & Giroux, 1968).

12. Maxine Hong Kingston, *The Woman Warrior: Memoirs of a Childhood Among Ghosts* (New York: Alfred Knopf, 1976).

13. Richard Henry Dana, *Two Years Before the Mast* (Boston, 1840).

14. Jelaluddin Rumi, "Quatrain 91," from *The Open Secret*, trans. by John Moyne and Coleman Barks (Putney, Vermont: Threshold Books, 1984).

Acknowledgments

So many have helped in the completion of these journeys, it would take pages to name them all. But I have to name a few, with special thanks. In Fukuoka, Thad and Shelby Nodine, Bob Norris and Shi-chan, and Sanae Hanada of the US Information Service. On Okinawa, Katsunori Yamazato of the University of the Ryukyus. On Bali, I Madé Surya and Judy Slattum, and Oka Wati of Ubud. In Hawai'i, Eddie and Myrna Kamae, Nona Beamer, Frank Stewart, and John Charlot of the University of Hawai'i, Jack Lockwood of the US Geological Survey, Dallas and Beverly Jackson, Jeannette Paulson, and Jane Yamashiro. And here on the mainland, Alan Cheuse, Jack Hicks, and Tom Christensen for believing in this book.

James D. Houston is the author of six novels and several nonfiction works, including *Californians: Searching for the Golden State,* which received an American Book Award from the Before Columbus Foundation. With Jeanne Wakatsuki Houston he coauthored *Farewell to Manzanar,* the story of her family's experience during the World War II internment. For the NBC teleplay based on this book they won the Humanitas Prize. Among his other honors are a Wallace Stegner Fellowship at Stanford, an NEA Fiction Grant, a PEN/Library of Congress Story Award, and a 1995 Rockefeller Foundation residency at Bellagio, Italy. A frequent visitor to the Asia/Pacific region, he has scripted four cultural documentary films in the Hawaiian Legacy Series, working with Honolulu director Eddie Kamae. He makes his home in Santa Cruz, California.